MORE ROGUE TRADERS

by Scott E.D. Skyrm

BROOKLYN
WRITERS PRESS

More Rogue Traders
All rights reserved

Copyright © 2018 by Scott E.D. Skyrm.

Published by the Brooklyn Writers Press in Brooklyn, New York.

ISBN: 978-1-7340973-5-1 (e-book)
ISBN: 978-0-9997903-4-2 (hardback)

Cover Design by: Kasya Ro

www.brooklynwriterspress.com

www.scottskyrm.com

ACKNOWLEDGEMENTS

I wish to thank Andrew Spencer, who is the best writing partner that anyone could ever have, thanks to Daniel J. McEvoy and for proofreading, Kasya Ro for an awesome book cover design, and for the never-ending support of my children: Paige, Harrison, and Spencer.

TABLE OF CONTENTS

PREFACE

I had left my office in Manhattan and boarded a train bound for my home in Connecticut. The ride from Grand Central to Connecticut typically takes about an hour, and I admit I often enjoy the time it takes to get there. It gives me a chance to decompress from the day's work before I get home to my family. Working as a senior manager in the fixed-income department of a subsidiary of a foreign bank, I split my time between sales calls and overseeing the handful of traders and salespeople who worked for me. It was a Friday in February and I was looking forward to a long weekend over the President's Day holiday. I closed my eyes and leaned back in my seat, letting the stress from the day wash away as the train sped northward.

My pastoral moment of calm wasn't long-lived, however. My phone rang. It was my boss' assistant and there was a problem at the office that required my immediate attention. One of the traders working under me – I'll call him Mr. Hill – had just informed him of a loss Hill had taken; the discussion took place right before the end-of-day reports were run. Given that I was in the business of buying and selling securities, losses aren't unheard of. Every trader, no matter how experienced and talented, has bad days when markets don't go the right way. But this was different.

Mr. Hill had worked at the bank for about five years. He was a very smart guy who knew his business, and he'd been successful in all of his job-related duties. He'd never given me any reason to doubt either his abilities or his honesty. He'd been hired to start an interest rate swaps trading business, a plan that had morphed into a Eurodollar futures trading business.

Eurodollars are technically U.S. dollar deposits that are held outside of the U.S., and based on the London Interbank Offered Rate (LIBOR) interest rate. There are futures contracts traded on Eurodollars that have a three-month maturity based off the three-month LIBOR rate. Each contract is worth a million dollars, and the futures contract is traded on the Chicago Mercantile Exchange.

Mr. Hill's trading strategy involved pricing the LIBOR interest rate yield curve, looking at the Eurodollar futures prices, then identifying which sectors of the curve were mispriced. For example, suppose there was a sudden surge of buying in the March Eurodollars futures contract. That buying would drive up the price of some contracts, but may not move the price of other Eurodollar contracts. The price spike creates a blip on the yield curve, and the price of the March futures contracts moves a little too high.

At that point, a savvy trader would sell the overpriced March contracts and, as a hedge, buy some other futures contracts that are similar. Then, wait for the March contract price to return to its normal place on the curve and unwind the trade. It might sound a little complex – and truth be told, it is – but when the right mind is at the controls, it's actually pretty simple. Unless, that is, things don't happen quite the way they're supposed to.

One problem in trading large and liquid futures contracts like Eurodollars is the specific rules governing the electronic trading environment. With this particular contract, trades are filled on a pro rata basis, meaning the fills are based on the size of the trader's individual order versus the overall amount that trades at the price level. For example, suppose there are 100 contracts being offered collectively and 10 of those contracts are yours. You are 10 of the 100 contracts. If a buy order comes in for 50 contracts, you are only entitled to sell half of what you were offering. That means you sell five contracts out of the 10 you wanted to sell.

Traders who operate in these high-volume futures contracts will often bid or offer for more than what they really want to trade. Using the above example, if you wanted to make sure you were able unload all 10 of your contracts, you might offer 20 contracts instead of just 10. Then, when the order came in for 50 contracts, your offer of 20 contacts is twice what was being offered before and you're entitled to sell 10 contracts, which was your original goal. Once the trade is complete and you're still left with 10 contracts offered, you just remove your order for the remaining 10 contracts and you're back to where you started.

However, there is an inherent risk to this trading method. Sometimes the market just doesn't do what it's supposed to. Let's say an order for 300 contracts came in while you were over-offering the 20 contracts. You only wanted to sell 10, but you just sold 20. Now you're short 10 additional contracts; a position that you didn't want to have. And, as a good trader, you never want to let the market put you in a trade that you don't want.

In Mr. Hill's case on that fateful February day, an anomaly hit the market. A trader somewhere had sent a sell order for 100,000 contracts. At $1 million per contract, that's a $100 billion transaction. Selling $100 billion worth of LIBOR interest rates either meant that someone expected very short-term rates to rise in the very near future, or some sort of banking crisis was pending. Alternatively, it might have just been that they were hedging risk from something else.

Given the state of the market at the time, the trader with the $100 billion sale was most likely betting on some type of event, something that would send bank rates skyrocketing. It happened to be one of the largest Eurodollar futures orders ever. Every single bid to buy Eurodollar futures contracts was immediately hit, and the market started dropping. Fast.

Mr. Hill was unlucky enough to be on the wrong side of the trade. When the order hit, he was trying to buy March contracts and sell the June contracts. Hoping to get a couple hundred contracts of the spread trade done, he was bidding for thousands of contracts. In other words, he was bidding for far more than he actually wanted, in the hopes of getting a much smaller order filled.

But then came the order for 100,000 contracts and Mr. Hill ended up owning the full amount of contracts that he was bidding for. At the same time, the market dropped as a result of the huge sale. He knew he had to do something, and do it quickly. He hit a few bids for both March and June contracts, selling some March contracts and some June contracts. It was good for him to unload whatever he could, even at a loss, but a hundred out of thousands of contracts was really just a drop in the bucket. Like I said, on a trading desk, these things happen to everyone.

Hill immediately sent another order, this time to sell his full position. But because of the falling market, there were few takers. He was able to sell a couple of contracts. A measly few. Over the course of the next few hours, he worked the markets, selling off contracts piecemeal. He hit whatever bids he could find, and offered contracts on any upswing in price, no matter how small. Finally, a large buy order for March futures – thousands of contracts – came in, and he hit the bid right away, booking a loss, but offloading much of his market risk. The trade helped to lift the market slightly and he was able to sell a few more contracts. Then he turned around and hit another bid for some more.

Right before 3:00 pm when the market was about to close, he was down to only a couple thousand March contracts, but he had oversold the June contracts in the process. He quickly balanced out his short by buying back some March contracts, which put him long some March contracts and short some June contracts as the trading day ended. At that point, his risk was very small. Yes, he stood the chance of losing money if June LIBOR rates moved higher, but the risk was mostly hedged and the trading day was over. He was ready to go home for the weekend, but first needed to tell somebody about what had happened. Everyone else on the trading floor was making their collective way out of the door, myself included, but he still kept quiet about it.

In the end, he didn't lose that much money. A change of one basis point in the price of Eurodollar futures is worth $25.00 on every contract. On 10,000 contracts, a drop of one basis point is a loss of $250,000. Granted, losing a few hundred thousand dollars stings, but in the grand scheme of things, it was manageable, simply because he could make it back in a relatively short period of time. Compared to some of the more monumental losses we'll see later, a few hundred thousand isn't even in the same category as a major loss.

The problematic part about Mr. Hill's trading escapades that day was that he didn't say anything to anyone while it was happening. Most likely, he expected to trade his way out of the loss, all the while hoping that his face didn't give anything away. And honestly, it didn't. I sat across from him the whole day, and I couldn't tell that anything was wrong. I had no way of knowing his loss was ten times his monthly loss limit, nor did I know that he was well over his trading limits.

At the time, our risk reports only took an end-of-day snapshot of trader's activities. In other words, only where he ended up at the end of the day. There was no way of knowing what route he had taken to get there. Those reports weren't run until everything was closed out at the end of the day. Mr. Hill figured he had until 5:00 pm to close out his oversized position, hopefully making his money back without anyone ever being the wiser.

With most of the facts in hand, the rest of the train ride was a time to consider Mr. Hill's future at the bank. Again, the loss wasn't staggering. We'd make it back easily within a short period of time. A part of me felt that he was just caught in a bad market; I'd experienced those myself. He did what he could to make the best of it. That part of me felt like Mr. Hill deserved a slap on the wrist. Let him do his job, which he was good at, and make the money back.

But another part of my brain started to speak louder, saying that I would be giving a rogue trader a do-over. I had always been fascinated with rogue traders, reading everything I could about their stories. I had read countless reports of how managers looked the other way while a trader literally pissed away hundreds of millions of dollars. Was I thinking about doing the same thing? If I gave him a second chance, wasn't I essentially saying that he hadn't done anything wrong, despite the fact that he'd violated company policy on several levels? And what's to say he wouldn't do it again, given that he certainly knew how to game the system?

Those questions banged around my overtaxed brain. The core of the problem, as I saw it, was that he hadn't said anything about it. If he'd told me, it would have been "our problem;" but by keeping it to himself, he made it "his problem." We could have worked together to figure out a solution, even if it meant taking a loss and moving on. But he didn't give me that option. A loss wasn't unforgivable, especially when it could be attributed to a freak occurrence; keeping it a secret, however, was. Mr. Hill had to go. Period.

With the decision made, at least in my mind, I tried once again to relax. But it was a futile exercise. Looking back now and knowing how rogue traders operate, all sorts of hypothetical situations materialize. What if he had input false swaps trades into the system that appeared as a hedge to his futures position? What if he'd been long something that wasn't as easy to price as futures contracts? Suppose he could manipulate the system and submit his own mark-to-market prices at the end of the day? Then he could show no loss at all. Suppose he'd been in charge of the back office at the same time he was working as a trader. He'd have been able to cover up the loss and nobody would have ever known about it.

He did, to his credit, admit to what he'd done at the end of the day. All of those hypotheticals that I consider today were just that, and none moved into the realm of reality. But that admission only came at a time when he didn't have another option. He was going to get caught, and he was hoping to soften the blow by coming clean and telling my boss' assistant about it. The more I thought about that fact, the more comfortable I was with the decision to fire him. I remembered a quote from the former Bear Stearns Senior Partner, Ace Greenberg, "The definition of a good trader is a guy who takes losses. The definition of an ex-trader is one who tries to cover up a loss."

As the train eased into the station in Connecticut, I thought I'd put the matter out of my mind for good. But the question still pops into my head and I've wrestled with it ever since. To this day, I still don't have the full answer. Was Mr. Hill a rogue trader?

As we shall see, his actions were eerily similar to those taken by other traders who weren't caught early enough. Those rogues managed to bring many firms in the financial industry to their knees, and the results were catastrophic for all involved.

ROBERT CITRON AND ORANGE COUNTY, 1994

On July 17, 1955, the famed businessman Walt Disney opened a theme park based on his animation empire in Anaheim, California called Disneyland. Promoters quickly proclaimed that it was "the happiest place on Earth." The park cost a staggering $17 million to build – an incredible amount of money at the time – and they expected so much additional highway traffic that it would require the addition of two lanes to Interstate 5. The first day the park opened, it was an invitation-only affair. Disney himself announced that day, "Disneyland is dedicated to the ideals, the dreams, and the hard facts that have created America, with the hope that it will be a source of joy and inspiration to all the world."

The general public was allowed to experience the happiest place the following day. Perhaps attendees were drawn by this promise of joy, the love of Disney, or perhaps just a desire for personal enjoyment. Whatever the reason, on the day the park officially opened, the line began to form at 2:00 in the morning and an estimated 50,000 visitors walked through the gates.

Disneyland's reputation grew by epic proportions. In 1959, when Russian Premier Nikita Khrushchev came to the United

States on an official state visit, despite the rising Cold War tensions, one of his few specific requests was to go to Disneyland. The park refused him entrance, however, because the head of America's cold-war adversary, The Soviet Union, might diminish the shine of "the happiest place on Earth."

Years later, Orange County, California, the home to Disneyland, co-opted the slogan the "happiest place on Earth" that was originally marketed by the theme park. Admittedly, Orange County has some credibility when it comes to claiming that lofty title. Located between Los Angeles and San Diego on the California coast, it covers approximately 790 square miles. The average annual temperature is 68° Fahrenheit, and the total average rainfall for the year is just twelve inches. In other words, the song is true – it really doesn't rain very often in Southern California.

The name of the county comes from sparling orange groves, which were once plentiful throughout the area. A fact that no doubt influenced John Steinbeck when he wrote in *The Grapes of Wrath*, "Why don't you go on west to California? There's work there, and it never gets cold. Why, you can reach out anywhere and pick an orange." Indeed, it never gets cold – nor hot, for that matter – and there's plenty of work to be found. In fact, with a population of 2.6 million and an unemployment rate of just 5%, it currently ranks as the fourth wealthiest county in the United States.

Although it is often described as a "wealthy white suburb," Orange County saw a large influx of Hispanics and Asians beginning in the 1980s, and together those minority groups comprised approximately one-third of the county's population by the mid-1990s. That racial division had created something of a political split in the county. North Orange County, which represented about 40% of the population, leaned Republican, favoring lower taxes in exchange for limited government services. South Orange County, however, which made up the remaining 60% of the population, tended to vote Democrat and supported increased government services and higher taxes to pay for them.

From the perspective of a unified whole, Orange County had a Republican majority, with approximately 52% of the voters supporting the GOP, 35% voting for the Democrats, and 13% describing themselves as independent. When pressed on the issues, a vast majority of voters considered themselves politically moderate – conservative on fiscal issues and liberal on social issues. One theme that held true, though, with a majority of the voters: They were adamantly opposed to new taxes because they felt that the money was not be put to good use, and, they held a deep distrust of elected officials.

Those elected country officials, however, were empowered by the state of California to provide a host of services. In addition to things like financing the sheriff, district attorney, county jails, school districts, and public transportation, the county officials were also in charge of the maintenance of parks, beaches, public works, and recreational facilities. All of that oversight took a staff of approximately 18,000 employees and a budget of approximately $3.7 billion a year. About one-third of that money came from property taxes.

Prior to 1978 in California, funding government services was a pretty easy job. If spending increased, officials just raised real estate and local sales taxes to offset the costs. There was no check on their authority. In essence, county officials had a blank check with endless reserves to finance their spending. However, after the severe inflation of the 1970s had pushed real estate taxes much higher, many residents – especially older retirees – could no longer afford to remain in the homes they'd purchased years before. After giving county officials a carte blanche for so long, residents were growing increasingly distrustful. Resentment grew and voters came to believe that there was too much waste in the government bureaucracy.

In 1978, taxpayers had decided that they'd had enough. Seeing runaway property taxes across California led to a citizens' initiative that was colloquially referred to as "The Taxpayers' Revolt." Its official name was the People's Initiative to Limit Property Taxation and is commonly referred to as Proposition 13. California voters approved Proposition 13 and amended the state constitution by a wide margin on June 6, 1978.

At its core, Proposition 13 imposed limits on a local government's ability to raise taxes, with a special focus on property taxes. It was established that any tax on property could not exceed 1% of the value of the property and increases beyond that amount required the approval of local voters, which needed to pass with a two-thirds majority. The new law severely restrained county officials' abilities to raise taxes and rolled back property assessments to the levels of 1975-1976.

Throughout the state, and especially in Orange County, political demands intensified from those who continued to want increased government services. Given the fact that voters were clearly not going to support a tax increase, the need for more county revenues was growing stronger, due to the increasing population and pressure on the county's infrastructure. In the end, with no way to increase taxes, it put increasing pressure on treasurers to realize greater returns on their investments.

In reaction to Proposition 13, a series of bills were passed to deregulate the county investment restrictions that were originally put in place. Prior to 1979, county treasurers were required to deposit excess county funds at banks. Those funds earned interest, of course, but bank deposit rates weren't nearly as high as other investments available at the time in the financial markets.

Over the course of the next thirteen years, the California state legislature continued to relax the investment rules for county treasurers. Gradually, municipalities were allowed to invest in such high-return investments as structured notes, derivatives, and even repo transactions that allowed them to leverage their investment portfolios. In 1981, Small Business Administration loans were allowed; commercial paper and bank CDs were deemed legal in 1983. The following year, the legislature relaxed the rules further, allowing treasurers to buy basic mortgage-backed securities (MBS), and then in 1986, medium-term corporate notes. By 1992, county treasurers were allowed to invest in collateralized MBS.

Over the course of those 13 years, county officials across the state successfully deregulated treasurers' investment rules, allowing them to find much higher returns on their excess cash. Of course, those higher returns also carried with them a higher degree of risk. And the leader of this movement was the Orange County treasurer and tax collector, a man named Robert Citron.

Robert Citron was the man who was delivering the high returns for Orange County and the one pushing for securities with higher returns at the state capital. The fact that he was proposing taking increased risks with the county's money didn't factor in to voters' thinking. In Orange County, the county's investment pool was morphing into the equivalent of a leveraged hedge fund. In the 1980s and early 1990s, Citron delivered the investment returns to cover approximately 35% of Orange County's operating budget. Taxes were low and services were being provided, so everybody was happy and life was grand. Until the bottom fell out.

As we have seen so many times before, there are always individuals who will find ways to exploit new laws. No matter how well-intended the laws or the benevolent motivations of those who seek to circumvent them. The story of Orange County, California, as it relates to the world of rogue traders, begins with the passage of Proposition 13. It ends, unfortunately, in the same place as so many other stories just like it: in bankruptcy, with Robert Citron driving the bus that took them there.

*　　*　　*

Robert Lafee Citron, born April 14, 1925, was not the prototypical rogue trader. He was a third-generation Californian, born in Los Angeles and raised in Burbank. His father, Jesse, was a homeopathic physician who claimed to have weaned the notoriously alcoholic W.C. Fields off of Scotch. Robert did not inherit his father's gift of self-aggrandizement, however. He attended the University of Southern California, where his course of study was pre-med. His car sported a vanity plate that read "LOV USC" and the horn played the university's fight song. But his love for the school didn't translate into academic success, as he never graduated.

His first job following his aborted college career was working as a consumer loan officer at Century Finance Corporation, a position that he held for nearly ten years. From there, he went on to join the Orange County tax collector's office and then, in 1971, he ran for the treasurer's job, a publicly-elected office. He won the election, and would be subsequently reelected to six consecutive terms.

The political success that he experienced was somewhat surprising, given he was a Democrat running for the office of tax collector in a staunchly Republican (and therefore anti-tax) county. He was a lifelong resident of Orange County, a fact that no doubt held some sway over voters. He was, interestingly enough, the only Democrat to hold elected office in Orange County at the time.

The position of treasurer in Orange County is officially referred to as treasurer–tax collector, which reflects the full scope of the job. It was a lucrative position for a government job – in 1994, the annual salary was $100,000 – but he wasn't one to spend money lavishly. He drove a Chrysler and ate lunch at the Elks Lodge, where his favorite meal was a soup and salad. He was also an active member of the Kiwanis Club and friends described him as

ROBERT CITRON AND ORANGE COUNTY, 1994

someone who was "always ready to lend a hand." He wore discount suits and turquoise jewelry, as well as a digital calculator watch. Again, clearly not the prototypical rogue trader.

He approached his job with something of a sense of humor. Citron was known to send out tax bills with slogans like "Taxes paid on time never draw fines" embossed across them. Co-workers described him as self-confident – a description that oftentimes was elevated to cocky – and they often called him "the wizard of high finance." That title, paired with his self-confidence, belied the fact that he had no education or background in finance whatsoever.

His job responsibilities included the collection of taxes (the tax collector part of the job), most of which was real estate tax, and the investment of excess cash in what was called the Investment Pool (the treasurer part of the job). Over the course of his twenty-four year reign as tax collector, Citron ruled his fiefdom without concern, because his power was essentially unchallenged by those around him. Much of that freedom was granted to him because of the eye-popping results he managed to produce. He delivered annual returns that, on average, were around 9%. When compared to the 5% the State of California was earning, Citron's results really made him look like a financial genius.

The Orange County Investment Pool existed to manage the revenues necessary to pay for things like capital improvements and operating expenses for the county. The Pool that Citron oversaw was a comingled fund, meaning that it was composed of the excess funds from all of the municipalities that were located in Orange County and pooled together. By doing so, those smaller local governments were able to participant in investments that were otherwise unavailable to them. It was, in a way, much like an individual investor buying shares in a mutual fund. Whereas a single investor might not have access to many institutional investments, a mutual fund has the combined resources of the many investors.

There were nearly 200 different municipalities' cash investments which made up the Investment Pool, which included school districts and other county agencies. In exchange for their services, the Orange County tax collector's office charged those municipal groups a .07% management fee, which was a spectacular deal for everyone involved. The investment returns far outweighed the fees, so the municipalities didn't complain. In fact, municipalities outside of Orange County were desperate to buy into the Investment Pool, but it was a closed fund. If you were outside the county, you were out of luck.

In theory, the Investment Pool was supposed to be governed by a conservative investment strategy. The guidelines stressed "safety and liquidity," and limited the maturity of the securities in the portfolio to no more than five years. In essence, it was supposed to be run like a money market fund, but the new deregulated restrictions failed to impose limits on the types of securities that could be held in the portfolio; there were no limits whatsoever in regards to a security's sensitivity to fluctuating interest rates; that is, how risky the securities could be.

A security's sensitivity to changes in interest rates is an important concept to understand because it's inherently linked to the bankruptcy of Orange County. A security's duration – the amount of time it takes for the coupon payments to fully payoff a bond – is also a measure to its sensitivity to changes in interest rates. In other words, because interest rates change over the course of a bond's lifespan, different bonds' prices will change more or less due to the changing yields in the market. In the case of the Investment Pool, the average maturity of the securities was only 1.4 years in 1992, however, the duration of those same securities – their sensitivity to interest rate changes – was 7.4 years. So the bonds, which were set to be paid in full in an average of 1.4 years, actually acted like much longer term securities.

For fifteen straight years, Citron's Investment Pool annual returns were nearly double those of the State of California's. With declining interest rates, the duration was clearly working in Citron's favor. In 1991, he had earned $60 million; in 1993, that number ballooned to $206 million. And all those great returns were going straight to the county and local municipalities who were sending as much money as they could back to Citron. So long as he continued to generate those numbers, he could have been investing in magic beans for all they cared. Whereas it wasn't the conservative money market style of investing that was required by the guidelines, nobody outside of Citron knew what was going on. They liked the returns, so they didn't ask too many questions.

It was fortunate for Orange County that Citron was producing the results that he was. During the early 1990s, there was an economic recession across the country and Orange County wasn't spared from the downturn. Between 1991 and 1993, the county lost approximately 57,000 jobs, and tax revenue took a steep nosedive. Luckily enough, however, Citron was delivering the extra income to cover the lost tax revenues, money that was desperately needed. In 1993, Citron was publicly praised by the Chairman of the Orange County Board of Supervisors "for the outstanding job you have done in guiding our financial ship through such turbulent times."

On the surface, it looked like Robert Citron was the answer to Orange County's financial prayers. But the reality was far different just below that surface. He had invested a lot of money in complex securities that, quite frankly, he didn't fully understand himself. And he didn't seem to grasp the fact that many of those securities were set up in such a way that they would stop paying interest when interest rates rose.

*   *   *

The portfolio in 1992 was heavily skewed with fixed-income government and corporate bonds, with about 58% of the holdings falling into that category. Inverse floating rate notes comprised another 26% of the portfolio, with cash and other investments making up the remainder. All told, the portfolio had $4 billion in structured notes, $2.5 billion of that had been leveraged via the repo market.

Most of the securities that Citron bought for the Investment Pool were government securities, which are issued by the United States government or the federal agencies. They include groups like Ginnie Mae, Fannie Mae, Freddie Mac, and the Federal Home Loan Banks. These bonds are either guaranteed out-right or at least had an implied guarantee by the full faith and credit of the United States. "Implied guarantee" means there was no actual government-issued guarantee for Freddie Mac, for instance. However, if an agency were teetering on the edge of default, it was widely assumed that the U.S. government would take it over and offer a financial bailout; exactly what happened in September 2008. Based on the possibility of default, agencys are as safe an investment as you can hope for, and perfect for something like a county investment pool geared towards conservative investment strategies.

When people looked at that portfolio and saw government-backed securities, they saw a safe, conservative portfolio. Those government guarantees against default gave the perception to the average voter that there was a 0% credit risk. In other words, it appeared that there was no chance of default and no scenario in which the bonds could lose money. But in reality, just looking at the credit risk failed to take into account the risk of changing interest rates. And, of course, there's always the maxim that tells us *any* investment – even one as presumably safe as bonds – can lose money.

In addition to the many standard fixed-income bonds in the portfolio, there were also structured bonds. Unless someone was a professional Wall Street trader, they might not fully understand the risk involved here. Just looking past the government agency issuer at the actual terms of the bond made a big difference. In the world of structured bonds, there were derivatives built into how the interest was paid.

Technically, a derivative in the fixed-income markets can be anything that's not a simple fixed-rate interest payment. Normal bonds pay a fixed-rate of interest for a fixed period of time – thus the "fixed income" label they're saddled with. Assuming there's no credit risk or risk of default, the holder knows exactly how much money they'll receive over the course of the bond's lifespan. It's such not a sexy way to way to make money, nor is it an easy way to make a lot of money, but it's dependable.

Things get a little more complex, however, when you start talking about structured notes. While a simple structured note can be something like a bond that pays a floating rate of interest. A Floating Rate Note (FRN), or a "floater" in market lingo, might pay a rate that is based on LIBOR and changes every six months. If Orange County, for example, owned a five-year FRN that paid LIBOR + 50 basis points, the payment might reset every six months for a total of five years to whatever LIBOR was plus an additional 50 basis points. Even though the person holding this security is locked into the investment for five years, they're always receiving a market rate, because the payment is constantly updated every six months. That can be a double-edged sword, however, because if interest rates go down, so does the amount of interest the bonds are paying.

Even FRNs can get a little complicated. One of the floaters in Orange County's portfolio was called an Inverse Swiss Floater. It was a structured note that paid off handsomely if the Swiss Franc declined in value and U.S. interest rates stayed relatively low. The key word here is "and." If only one of those things happened, the interest rate on the bond was basically the same as LIBOR. In the event neither of those things happened, the bond paid no interest whatsoever.

An even more complicated structure in the Investment Pool was what's called a range note. That's a bond that pays a very attractive interest rate, so long as interest rates stayed within a certain range. Range notes are very complex investment products, and they're wildly speculative. Buyers are betting that interest rates will remain relatively the same for the life of the bond, which is something that is very difficult for anyone – even financial wizards – to predict. For example, a range note that Orange County owned paid a 5.00% interest rate as long as LIBOR remained between 3.00% and 4.00%. If LIBOR moved below or above the range, the bond paid no interest at all.

Twenty-six percent of the Investment Pool consisted of inverse floating-rate notes, which were even more complicated than regular floaters. The strategy behind the inverse floating rate note is that that interest rates will not rise. That much is pretty easy, but the formula can be anything but easy to understand. A typical formula might be that the interest rate on the bond is 7.00% minus LIBOR, with a reset every six months. So if LIBOR was trading at 3.00%, the inverse floater would pay a rate of 4.00% (7.00%-3.00%). But if LIBOR shot up to 6.00% six months later, then that same note would only pay 1.00% (7.00%-6.00%). An inverse floater can be very speculative and it's extremely sensitive to changing interest rates.

Something that's very important about structured notes is that there's a very limited secondary market. Many are put together in such a way that they are incredibly complicated, so if you want to sell them before maturity, it's going to be difficult and you're probably looking at selling them at a discount and probably taking a loss.

Citron, however, wasn't put off by any of them, nor was he worried about the limited secondary market. He brushed off the risk when describing over a quarter of his portfolio, "Inverse floaters are indexed to produce a higher yield when interest rates remain steady or decline." Two-out-of-three ain't bad, we're told. But what happens when rates go up? Conveniently – or perhaps naively – he just left out that third option.

Another fact about the Orange County Investment Pool is that it was leveraged - billions of its holdings were financed through repo transactions. Often called "the plumbing of the financial system," the repo market is one of the largest financial markets in the world, but remains a mystery to most investors. Essentially, repo – short for repurchase agreement – is a tool to leverage one's holdings. An investment portfolio loans the securities they own – in the case of Orange County they owned bonds – as collateral for a cash loan. At its core, repo is a collateralized loan. The borrower gets a short-term loan and they put up their securities as a guarantee against default.

By loaning securities to Wall Street banks through repo transactions, Orange County was able to borrow money to purchase more securities. That's the leverage component of the equation. They would have to pay back the loan with interest in order to get their collateral back. "We have perfected the reverse-repo procedure to new levels," Citron bragged. It was quite the boast for a man with no professional experience in the financial markets about a financial product that few outside of the financial industry truly understood.

The thing about leverage, as we've seen so often before, is that it's a great way to magnify your profits. It's a gamble that many investors take daily. If you double your holdings, you double your returns, assuming that the securities increase in value. But again, the opposite also holds true. If you double your holdings, you double your losses if the securities decline in value.

Just as Citron wasn't concerned about the potential losses from higher interest rates, he didn't appear overly concerned with his leveraged positions either. He was, at his peak, carrying about

$20.6 billion in assets, with only approximately $7.6 billion of actual cash in the Investment Pool. He had borrowed upwards of $13 billion to buy more securities, most of which were tied to the belief that interest rates would either stay the same or decline. In market parlance, Orange County was leveraged about 2.7 to 1 (20.6 billion divided by 7.6 billion). That ratio was magnified further by the fact that the structured securities created even more leverage. Those securities were built in such a way that the payouts were high for the winners and very low for the losers. Leveraging structured notes to buy more structured notes carries both a tremendous amount of risk and reward.

*   *   *

Throughout his reign as the king of Orange County's finances, Citron enjoyed a great deal of independence. Hand-in-hand with that independence went a lack of accountability from the Board of Supervisors. His returns spoke for themselves. He was making plenty of money, so there appeared to be no reason to question his methods. As the old saying goes, "If it isn't broken, don't fix it." It was just easier to blindly accept his results without questioning him. Perhaps there was an unspoken fear that if they looked behind the curtain, they would find that the great and powerful Citron had no idea what he was doing. But then, of course, no one else in country government understood what he was doing either.

And truth be told, the man behind the curtain wasn't applying any kind of professional strategy when it came to picking investments. It wasn't until 1988 when former White House Chief of Staff Donald Regan informed the nation that then-First Lady Nancy Reagan was consulting an astrologer on a regular basis. The national reaction was a mixture of horror and hilarity that the woman who slept next to the president actually believed in astrology. That same reaction should have materialized in Orange County when it came to light that Robert Citron was also consulting an astrologer. Specifically, he used a "star chart" that he purchased for $4.50 from an astrologer in Indianapolis to help guide his investing. He claimed that he used it for clues about upcoming market events.

But, as it turned out, not everyone was fooled by Bob Citron; the investment banks began to sound the alarm about his positions back in 1992. Merrill Lynch's risk management group prepared an in-depth analysis of Orange County's portfolio and the findings were not very complimentary. The main issue was that the Investment Pool was carrying far too much exposure to rising interest rates. Michael Stamenson, the Merrill Lynch salesman who covered the Orange County account, shared the report with Citron, who was completely unmoved by its findings.

The following year, in February 1993, the head of Merrill's derivatives group wrote a memo in which he recommended that Orange County reduce their risk and sell $2.8 billion of their structured notes. Then, in March, Merrill offered to purchase $3.5 billion of the structured notes, a sale that would have netted the Investment Pool a cool $100 million in profit. Interest rates were, at the time, very low as the federal funds target rate was set at 3.00%, so it made sense that the fund should show a tidy profit. And, of course, Merrill stood to make a great deal of money themselves by getting Orange County out of the trades they put them into in the first place.

Perhaps it was a moment of financial insight – or perhaps it was the star chart – that led Citron to decline the proposal. Whatever his motivation, it was his final decision. He was not going to sell anything. Then, Merrill followed-up by putting the proposal in writing. Citron again refused. Merrill continued to communicate with Citron about the risks he was taking and Citron continued to take no action.

That same year, Goldman Sachs openly criticized the amount of risk in the Investment Pool in a research report. After reading it, Citron was enraged. Rather than seriously consider the opinions of a professional investment bank – opinions that echoed another professional investment bank – Citron went on the defensive and penned a letter back, in which he said, "Goldman does not understand the type of investment strategies that we are using. I would suggest you not seek doing business with Orange County."

An oft-reference Biblical quote warns, "Pride comes before destruction, and an arrogant spirit before a fall." It is a lesson that has been played out since the dawn of time and it happens quite often in the financial world. Citron would have been wise to heed the warnings, but his own self-assurance blinded him to what was happening around him. His perceived successes were contained inside a house made of straw, and a very big, very bad storm was about to hit the markets.

*   *   *

The storm in question came in the form of higher interest rates. As 1994 dawned, the Orange County Investment Pool was a disaster waiting to happen. For the entire year of 1993, the Federal Reserve had kept short-term interest rates at 3.00%. Most investors and financial institutions alike had grown accustomed to the low rates and expected the Fed to keep things unchanged for an extended period of time, but that was all about to change. On February 4, 1994, the Fed raised short-term interest rates to 3.25%, an action that spooked the markets. Because they had issued very little warning, a massive sell-off in the fixed-income markets ensued.

Throughout the year, the overnight federal funds rate shot up from 3.00% in January of 1994 all the way to 5.50% in November, a massive spike in such a relatively short period of time. The U.S. Treasury Ten-Year Note followed, skyrocketing from a 5.80% rate in February to over 8.00% in November of that year. These rising interest rates led to a series of high-profile bankruptcies, including Kidder Peabody and Askin Capital Management. But throughout the year, Citron was unfazed. He kept buying more and more bonds, adding to his bets that were already proving to be losers.

In the spring of 1994, the election season was in full-swing and Robert Citron was facing off against John Moorlach for the office of Orange County Tax Collector. During the campaign, Citron was predictably self-congratulatory. "I wrote the law," he reminded his constituents about deregulating county investment regulations fifteen years earlier, "and I'm getting the best returns in the state." He described himself in the press as the 68-year-old "dean of county officials." Several newspapers referred to him as "a nationally-recognized money manager" who had "generated billions of dollars in tax relief for local taxpayers." He seemed to be the dream candidate for the job.

Moorlach countered with his own attacks on the incumbent. He was a 38-year-old accountant who was a partner in his firm and a local Republican Party official. Given the political leanings of Orange County, not to mention that he had certified financial train-ing and experience with taxation, it would make sense that he'd be a shoo-in for the office. Moorlach predicted that a financial disas-ter was looming, a storm of massive proportions that was created by Citron's liberal use of leverage and the purchase speculative securities. He promised to unwind Citron's Gordian Knot of risky investments and, though it might result in an initial loss, it would return the county to a conservative and safe financial situation. He sounded a little bit like Chicken Little claiming that the sky was falling, but he had sound evidence to back up his claims.

Truth was the enemy of the candidate, however, and hyperbole won the day. Residents of Orange County didn't seem to care about things like risk exposure and financial doomsdays. That's what their tax collector was supposed to worry about and it seemed Citron had been doing an excellent job managing those things so far. In the end, Citron won 61% of the vote, compared to Moorlach's 39%, and kept his office for another term. It would be his last.

While still riding the wave of support that had ushered him into office for his seventh term, Citron modified the holdings in the Investment Pool. He ramped up the inverse floater positions to $6.6 billion, which now represented 32% of the overall portfolio. Other structured notes dropped to a mere $1.7 billion (8% of the portfolio) with standard fixed-income investments still making up the bulk of the remainder of the portfolio at $9.7 billion, or 47%.

But as interest rates were rising, the effects on the Investment Pool were devastating. On May 31, 1994, the Pool had lost an estimated $1.2 billion. The rising rates meant that many of the structured notes and inverse floaters were paying no interest at all, and even those that were still paying weren't returning very much. Compounding that was the fact that he had to come up with increasingly more cash as margin for his repo loans.

Margin calls are never good for an investor to get, because it means that the value of the securities has fallen to the point that there's no longer enough collateral in the account. When a financial institution issues a margin call, it means someone has to come up with the extra cash quickly. Ideally, Orange County would have a cash reserve that they could tap to meet the margin calls, but they already exhausted it. Alternatively, they could sell securities to generate cash, but that would means booking a loss on their already devalued holdings. By the middle of 1994, Orange County had received margin calls totally approximately $300 million. Less money was coming while more was going out. The ship was taking on water and there was nothing to plug the hole with.

Then, things went from bad to worse for Citron. Citron – working together with Matthew Raabe, the Orange County assistant treasurer – calculated that the Investment Pool had suffered $1.5 billion in losses due to the rising interest rates. It was a catastrophic loss on so many levels. No investor likes to lose money, especially when you're talking about losses with the word billion in them. But these losses were more than just a bank or hedge fund losing money on behalf of already wealthy investors seeking to make themselves just a little wealthier. It was the operating capital for the entire county. It represented salaries for employees, schools for kids, and public services for residents. Citron knew he had to do something to keep things afloat, so, in a last-ditch effort to save both himself and his image, he and Raabe decided to hide the losses.

They moved $80 million in cash out of the accounts of the smaller municipalities and into Orange County's own accounts. Citron then transferred securities from the Orange County General Fund – money that was used to pay for county expenses – into the Investment Pool, effectively diverting money from school districts to the county. It was an illegal transfer on his part. The money would be used to cover the losses and the margin call requests that were becoming ever-more frequent. Much like leveraging the fund had precipitated his destruction, his strategy of robbing Peter to pay Paul was just digging his hole a little deeper.

The pair began keeping two sets of financial records. One book had the inflated numbers that were shown to the public, clearly a much rosier picture than reality. The other book documented the illegal transfers, money that Citron knew, on some level, they'd have to pay back at some point. Mimicking the actions of other rogue traders, he convinced himself that this was a stop-gap, just a quick fix to get past a bump in the road. Once the market came back, he'd put the money back and nobody would ever know. The truth, though, the value of the fund was rapidly declining.

By that fall, the Pool was essentially insolvent. But Citron refused to acknowledge reality, at least publicly. He clung to the belief that the losses the Pool had sustained were only "paper losses," meaning that until the securities were sold, they didn't actually exist. He patently refused to alter his mindset when asked about it, essentially sticking his head in the sand and claiming he couldn't see any problems. Raabe, for his part, continued to tow the party line despite the crumbling walls around him. He assured the local municipalities that there was plenty of cash-on-hand withdrawals. He later said that Citron "was an imposing dominating figure all throughout the county for many, many, many years." But as the losses mounted, Citron's appearance changed. According to Raabe, "By November 1994, he was this fragile old man."

On December 1, 1994, Orange County publically acknowledged that the Investment Pool had lost $1.64 billion. In truth, that number was still overly optimistic, but it was the first time that anyone publically admitted that something was wrong. The number, though conservative, amounted to nearly $1,000 for every resident of Orange County. It was as if a bomb had gone off in the middle of the happiest place on Earth, and nobody knew exactly how to react.

Raabe was called into a secret meeting with county officials where he offered a candid view into the office of the tax collector. "Bob had a mail-order astrologist that gave him interest rate predictions," he told the officials, "and a psychic that he consulted." Upon hearing that, the question was posed to the Orange County counsel whether Citron "was competent to be doing what he was doing." The meeting adjourned after a brief discussion regarding Citron's future. The unanimous verdict was that the tax collector had to resign immediately.

Members of the Board of Supervisors visited Citron at his home immediately following the meeting with Raabe and asked him about his reliance on astrology and a psychic. It's almost comical to imagine their reaction when they heard Citron's claim that he had stopped consulting his star chart, which was the reason why his strategy had collapsed. The officials immediately asked for his resignation.

On December 4, 1994, at the age of 69, Robert Citron resigned as the tax collector for Orange County. "After much thought and soul-searching and with much regret," he said in his announcement, "I have decided, for the benefit of the County of Orange, to resign." In his place, Mathew Raabe was named acting treasurer.

Two days later, on December 6, news of the problems in Southern California made their way to the East Coast. Credit Suisse First Boston demanded repayment of $2 billion of its repo loans and immediately seized $1.25 billion of Orange County's securities. That would be the first domino to fall that day.

At 4:52 PM Pacific Time later that day, Orange County, California, declared bankruptcy, making it the largest municipal bankruptcy in the history of the United States.

★   ★   ★

Declaring bankruptcy in the real world is not quite the same as doing so in a game of Monopoly. In the board game, when you declare bankruptcy, it means you're completely out of cash and unable to pay the required rent due to the player on whose property you landed on. In the overall scheme of things, it that can be quickly rectified by mortgaging or selling your property.

In the United States, however, the legal definition of a bankruptcy can vary significantly. In the case of Orange County, when they declared bankruptcy, it was not indicative of the typical kind of insolvency. In fact, they had approximately $650 million in cash-on-hand at the time, but they had potential liabilities that far exceeded that amount. When the county declared Chapter 9 bankruptcy to seek protection, they thought they were stopping a situation that resembled a run on a bank. By seeking protection under the bankruptcy laws, their intention was to prevent a run on the Investment Pool – their personal bank, so to speak – by the investment banks seeking the repayment of their repo loans and the smaller municipalities who had invested in the Pool.

Chapter 9 bankruptcy is a specific type of reorganization reserved solely for municipalities facing the situation that Orange County was in the middle of. Up until the Great Depression, it was assumed that if a municipality was no longer able to pay its bills, they could just raise taxes on the people living within their boundaries. But in 1934, when the country was mired one of the greatest economic disasters in history, raising taxes wasn't an option. The populace just didn't have the money to pay, but they still needed government services. So when the Bankruptcy Act came into being, a part of it was called Chapter 9 and it gave bankruptcy protection to municipalities. Up until Orange County invoked the law, it was a rarely-used. When it was, it had only been invoked by small rural cities and districts that few Americans had ever heard of. The Orange County bankruptcy was an epic, unprecedented financial collapse.

Chapter 9, like other types of bankruptcy, has specific rules and parameters for those seeking protection. To qualify under Chapter 9, the entity must be an insolvent municipality, meaning an incorporated residential district that cannot afford to pay its debts. When Chapter 9 protection is in place, the debtor must negotiate with its creditors in good faith to find a mutually-agreeable solution to the debt situation.

A very important feature of Chapter 9 is that the law specifically does not include Section 559 of the larger bankruptcy code. Section 559 allows a repo counterparty to liquidate repurchase agreements in order to recoup their money. In other words, whereas the whole repo market is set up so that a creditor can sell the collateral in the event of default, Chapter 9 bankruptcy prohibits – or at least doesn't explicitly allow – that to happen. It was, at the time, an untested loophole in the law. Orange County officials were pinning their hopes that by declaring Chapter 9, their repo counterparties would have their hands tied and wouldn't be able to liquidate the securities they were holding.

That was one part of the two-fold rationale for declaring bankruptcy. The other was to prevent a run on the Investment Pool funds by the smaller municipalities that had invested their money with the county.

Ironically – and perhaps predictably – when Orange County filed for bankruptcy, the result was the exact opposite. The Wall Street firms interpreted the bankruptcy filing as a default, which it was, and began to enforce the terms of the repo agreements. That meant they all began liquidating Orange County's positions.

Merrill was the next one to launch a liquidation salvo, selling off all of $800 million in securities that they were holding from repo financing. That action resulted in an initial profit of $40 million for Merrill, but that number was slashed down to just $8 million after expenses and lost profits were deducted. The bank contented that they were legally allowed to sell off the securities, because the repo legal agreement allowed for liquidation in the event of a default. Per general bankruptcy law, repo agreements are exempt from being frozen, which means they can be seized and sold by the creditor.

The Orange County Board of Supervisors begged to differ and they authorized their lawyers to begin filing lawsuits against any Wall Street firm that liquidated securities. They alleged that selling collateral was illegal under the Chapter 9 because there was no mention of repo agreements in the law. Banks were, therefore, legally obligated to return the securities to Orange County. Their argument, though legally clever, fell on deaf ears and the liquidations proceeded.

On December 8, the county defaulted on $110 million in notes that were due, prompting a downgrade in their credit rating. Residents of Orange County were nervous – media reports had pinned the losses ranging from $2 billion up to $3 billion, depending on which rumor was circulating – but county officials assured them there would be no impact whatsoever on police, fire, and paramedic services. Those were sacred cows and would be funded no matter what. One resident who spoke at a meeting of the Board of Supervisors asked the question that everyone else was wondering: "When's the last time a major issuer that was AA-rated was put on credit watch and filed for bankruptcy in the space of four days?"

Given the unprecedented nature of Orange County's situation, the answer to that question was simple: Never.

Adding insult to injury, Orange County became the butt of jokes and late-night talk show monologues. The self-proclaimed happiest place on Earth was now the "poor little rich county," and more than one comic suggested that Bob Citron had changed the name of Orange County to Lemon County. Ironically, his last name is the French word for lemon, so the joke was fitting on multiple levels.

Soon after, the Orange County district attorney's office issued search warrants for Citron's office. The entire area was cordoned off with yellow crime scene tape, as a team of 30 investigators arrived. They carted off enough documents that fill two vans and seized all of the computers in the office.

While the investigation was getting started, the county still faced the task of liquidating the remainder of their portfolio. At of the beginning of January 1995, they still had 206 securities left and county officials hired Salomon Brothers to advise them on the liquidation. The riskiest securities were sold-off at a public auction, with many of the others sold in the traditional market.

The holdings were to be pared down to the barest of bones. Those securities remaining consisted of approximately $1.9 billion in regular corporate- and government-issued fixed-rate debt, which were truly plain-vanilla investments. There was still $2.8 billion in basic structured notes that were far from the complex derivatives that Citron had been in love with just a few months earlier. In addition, there was still between $200 to $300 million in cash. Going forward, the county announced that the Investment Pool would only buy basic securities. The returns would no longer be the subject of envy, but they'd be consistent. The restructuring, as far as the Investment Pool was concerned, was complete.

After the flaws in the Investment Pool had been corrected – and in a very short timeframe, no less – you might think that the cloud over Orange County had gone away. However, both Moody's and Standard & Poor downgraded the county's debt to junk bond status, meaning there was a good probability that the county might default on any bonds it issued. Potential buyers were understandably wary of acquiring any new Orange County debt.

Robert Citron had remained relatively quiet about the whole situation following his sudden departure, but on January 17, 1995, he publicly blamed the Investment Pool's collapse on the investment banks that had sold him the securities in the first place. The man who'd campaigned on his successes and had embraced the moniker of "wizard of high finance" was suddenly changing his stance. Gone was the bravado of the man who made it rain money, replaced by a finger-pointing neophyte. Citron claimed he was "an inexperienced investor," and Merrill Lynch had led him astray.

What followed was a game of finger-pointing which almost requires a roadmap to follow. Democrats railed against their Republican counterparts for passing Proposition 13 in the first place; as that law had limited the county's ability to increase taxes. Republicans, in turn, pointed a finger at the Board of Supervisors, who had failed to oversee the treasurer and monitor what he was doing. The Board of Supervisors blamed Citron for buying the securities, and Citron blamed Merrill Lynch for selling him the securities. Round-and-round it went, but nothing changed the fact that Orange County had devolved from an enviable upper-class enclave to the largest municipal bankruptcy in the history of the United States.

On March 7, William J. Popejoy was named the interim chief administrative officer for Orange County. He was well-known throughout the area as a wealthy resident and a successful businessman. He seemed like the ideal choice to right the ship, given his business experience. His first official action was to terminate Matthew Raabe from his position of acting treasurer and followed up by proposing a massive round of belt-tightening and budget cuts.

The plan Popejoy put forward was austere. He proposed laying-off 1,040 county employees and leaving 563 proposed jobs vacant. That combination came with it a projected savings of $80 million in the annual budget. He also proposed selling county assets, which included facilities like public libraries, correctional institutions, various government buildings, a 7.7-acre parking lot, and the John Wayne Airport. Collectively, those assets would net the county somewhere around $100 million. He then suggested opening up landfills to neighboring communities; essentially allowing the affluent community to become a garbage repository of other towns. Finally, on March 15, he proposed raising the sales tax from 7.75% to 8.25%.

County residents were outraged by the proposals and felt Popejoy was going a little too far. Cutting services and raising taxes? That was too much. Three members of the Board of Supervisors received bomb threats at their homes. But because of Proposition 13, voters had to approve the proposed sales tax increase and, when the results were tallied, the measure failed miserably, garnering only 39% of the votes. Residents didn't want – were adamantly opposed to – budget cuts, the sale of county assets, or increases in sales tax. County residents, in no way, wanted to pay for the losses. The only option left was to borrow money to fund the losses, so that's exactly what the county decided to do.

Orange County officials worked with the local governments and school districts that had money tied up in the Investment Pool to pay them back. They struck a deal on March 17 to pay back those municipalities in installments. First, they'd get 77 cents on the dollar up-front and the remaining 23 cents would be paid later from money generated from the bond issue. In other words, the original belt-tightening that Popejoy had proposed just wasn't going to happen.

On March 23, the county announced that it planned to sell $750 million worth of new debt in order to cover the losses. The bond issue would be secured by new motor vehicle license fees, as well as by revenues generated by the county landfills. The county ended up issuing $880 million in bonds, but because of they were classified as junk bonds now, the yields they paid were much higher than normal. The sentiment among bond buyers was that Orange County could pay its debts, but they just didn't want to. As it stands now, the debt they issued in 1995 won't be fully paid-off until 2017.

John Moorlach, who lost to Citron in the election, suddenly saw his reputation as a financial prognosticator grow exponentially. He was the only person who publicly predicted that Orange County was headed for trouble, something that not even the most pessimistic of predictors had foreseen. He was appointed the new Orange County treasurer without an election and would later go on to be elected to the county's Board of Supervisors and eventually become chairman of that governing body.

In explaining what had happened to the Investment Pool, Moorlach was straightforward, demonstrating a keen understanding of the risks that Citron had either ignored or simply failed to understand: "It really wasn't the derivatives that caused the problem," he said. "Those were just the sleeping pills. The leverage was the alcohol, and you just don't mix the two."

*　　*　　*

Following the Orange County bankruptcy, it was widely expected that derivatives would be put under an intense microscope during the Senate Banking Committee hearings on the incident. Derivatives weren't a new investment tool at the time, but they had almost exclusively been reserved for savvy investors who knew the market and the risks involved. In the case of Robert Citron, none of those qualities were true. He was a naïve and inexperienced investor who chased potential returns while turning a blind (or ignorant) eye that he could lose a great deal of money.

However, the Republican-controlled Congress placed the blame at the feet of Citron, not the risky securities that were the foundation of his strategy. In other words, the cracked bricks weren't to blame for the house falling down. It was the fact that the builder had chosen to use them. Then-Chairmen of the Federal Reserve Alan Greenspan testified before Congress that "it would be a grave error to demonize derivatives or blame them for the loss." He went on to say that the losses sustained by the Orange County Investment Pool were "a necessary price we have to pay for what is a valuable addition to our financial system."

Orange County was seen as collateral damage. The situation was created by voters choosing a man who didn't know what he was doing and they made the bed they were lying in. The Senate

Banking Committee decided that increased regulation of derivatives was not warranted at the time.

But that failure of Congress to act didn't mean Citron and his lackey Raabe were getting off without some sort of punishment. They had, after all, overseen the virtual financial destruction of one of the wealthiest counties in the United States. The pair was charged with misallocating more than $200 million and they were indicted by a grand jury on April 27, 1995.

Given the charges that he was facing, Citron faced a possible prison sentence of 14 years and a maximum fine of $10 million, Citron's attorney begged for leniency, citing the fact that his client was frail and in ailing health. Citron had, they argued, believed himself to be acting in the best interests of the county. Any illegal actions on his part were because he just didn't know any better. His heart, if not his brain, had been in the right place. The prosecutors gave in, and dropped their demand to a seven-year prison sentence and a $400,000 fine.

After further negotiations, Citron agreed to plead guilty to six separate felony counts, including misappropriating funds, making a false statement to sell Orange County securities, making false bookkeeping entries, and shifting money between accounts. "I committed a felony," he admitted in court, "with the assistance of Matthew Raabe." As a part of his plea deal, he agreed to fully cooperate against others involved, including Raabe.

On November 19, 1996, Citron was sentenced to one year in a work-release program and ordered to pay a $100,000 fine. He was given the opportunity to participate in the program because of his poor health and ended up only serving nine months of his sentence. During his time, he worked at the sheriff's commissary, where he alphabetized prisoner requests for deodorant, envelopes, candy bars, and other assorted items available for purchase.

Matthew Raabe was charged with five felony counts and decided to take his chances in court rather than accept a plea. The trial began in April 1997 and Citron was called as a witness for the prosecution. On the stand, he accused Raabe of developing and instituting the plan whereby they took almost $90 million of investors' money. When combined with other testimony, Citron helped secure a guilty verdict against his former assistant on all five charges. Raabe was sentenced to three years in prison, but the conviction was later overturned on appeal in 2001 and thrown out. Despite promises by the prosecution to retry him, Raabe has yet to return to court.

While the men who had overseen the financial collapse of Orange County were on trial, the county itself was working to regain the money they had lost by suing the banks that had sold them the securities. It was, to many minds, a bizarre and misguided attempt to portray the banks as the criminals in the bankruptcy. Akin to blaming a liquor manufacturer for "forcing" a person to drink too much, Orange County claimed that the banks should have known better than to sell securities to Citron because he didn't know what he was doing.

In the first lawsuit, filed in January of 1995, Merrill Lynch was sued for $3.6 billion in restitution and $2 billion in damages. The county accused Merrill of "wantonly and callously" selling them high-risk securities and went so far as to say that Citron had actually lacked the legal authority under California's state constitution to buy the securities in the first place. Those same laws that Citron himself helped to write. To that point, they were correct, as the constitution specifically forbade any municipality from incurring debt that exceeded a year's worth of revenues without approval of two-thirds of county voters. In other words, Merrill Lynch was being sued because Citron had violated the law.

As absurd as the lawsuit might have sounded, Merrill didn't take the charges lightly and fought back. They produced documents showing they had, in fact, warned the county about its level of risk, including copies of the documents they'd sent to Citron. They pointed out that their Chief Risk Officer had visited with Citron in person in February of 1992 and they had even offered to buy back some of the securities in 1993.

The bank argued that they believed they were dealing with a man who was a sophisticated investor, understood the risks he was taking, and that he was operating with full transparency as far as the public was concerned. In the end, Merrill settled out of court and paid $434 million to Orange County, though the bank maintained that they were not at fault in any way.

Other Wall Street banks followed the trail blazed by Merrill, settling out of court with the county's lawyers. The targets included such Wall Street titans as Morgan Stanley, Smith Barney, Credit Suisse First Boston, Bear Stearns, among others. By the time the lawsuits had all been settled, Orange County had successfully negotiated nearly $595 million in addition to the Merrill settlement.

But Orange County wasn't done yet. They set their sights on KPMG Peat Marwick, the accounting firm responsible for auditing the county's finances. They charged that the firm had failed to warn the county officials about the nature of the investments, specifically the volatility and high risk. Under county rules, the Board of Supervisors was required to review the investment portfolio after a KPMG analysis and they claimed they were never afforded that chance. KPMG would settle for $75 million in 1998.

All told, Orange County was awarded more than $1.1 billion from the various targets of their lawsuits.

In the ultimate ironic twist to this whole story, Merrill Lynch commissioned an analysis of the Orange County Investment Pool and the results were released on April 25, 1996. The analysis was compiled by renowned economist and Nobel Laureate Merton Miller. In his report, Miller stated, "Our analysis shows that if bankruptcy had not been declared, the value of the Orange

County Investment Pool portfolio would have increased by about $1.8 billion between December 1, 1994, and March 29, 1996."

In other words, had the county held onto the securities and ridden out the storm, they would have made all their money back. Of course, it's easy to say that years after the fact with the benefit of perfect hindsight. At the time, there was a widely-held belief that the Fed would continue raising rates and higher rates would have exacerbating the Investment Pool's losses. But as it happened, in the second half of 1995, the Federal Reserve stopped raising interest rates. The Orange County bankruptcy had come at the worst possible time, when interest rates were at their highest.

Yes, it's easy to look back and say that county officials should have waited. For them to have sat idle seemed like the opposite of what they should have done. In hindsight, they should have acted sooner, and truth be told, had they done nothing, they would have been criticized for not dealing with the situation. But it does serve to illustrate a very powerful truth on Wall Street. Bad markets are inevitable, but so are good markets. People who suffer the most in investing are often the ones who rely on emotional, knee-jerk reactions. And apparently the ones who rely on astrology for investment advice.

*　　*　　*

Following the Orange County debacle, the California state legislature rewrote the state's investment guidelines that had been changed following the passage of Proposition 13. The new rules restricted county treasurers' investment options, especially in terms of the amount of risk they were allowed to assume. County fund investment objectives were codified so that safety of principal was the primary goal. Liquidity needs of the depositor and the investment return came in second and third. Inverse floaters and structured securities were specifically prohibited.

The county was able to recover from what was, at the time, the largest municipal bankruptcy in history in just 18 months, emerging from protection in June of 1996. Approximately 3,000 county jobs were cut from the budget over the next few years.

Citron never took full responsibility for his actions in bringing Orange County to financial collapse, choosing instead to blame his subordinates and Wall Street bankers. As close as he came to admitting guilt was saying, "In retrospect, I find that I wasn't the sophisticated treasurer that I said I was." That admission, however, did not prompt him to forego his county pension. By 2013, with cost-of-living increases factored in, that pension paid him $150,000 a year. In January of that year, however, he died at St. Joseph Hospital in Orange, California, the victim of a heart attack.

What really brought on Citron's downfall in the end wasn't so much his failure to understand the investments, but rather the fact that he was trying to do the impossible. It's an appealing prospect as a citizen to receive increased government services without having to pay for them. Many politicians over the years have promised to do exactly that. Unfortunately, however, few manage to deliver.

The voters of Orange County weren't unlike voters everywhere, in that they wanted that elusive combination for themselves. And like a Heaven-sent gift, there was Robert Citron promising to give it to them. What's more, he managed to make good on that promise for a long period of time. Orange County's inability to finance their government with a tax increase – something that was restricted by Proposition 13 – forced them to find other ways to pay their bills. Citron was under immense pressure to generate revenues and that pressure led him to do things that were incredibly risky and, ultimately, self-destructive. Ironically, he had spearheaded the law that brought him down in the end.

Citron's story is unique in that he wasn't the typical rogue trader. He wasn't trying to score the corner office or a seven-figure bonus. In his mind, he was just trying to pay for the government services for his constituents. But at the same time, his story is not unique in the world of rogue traders. Granted, the large bonuses that are so often associated with Wall Street were not there, but the same underlying pressures to perform were. The same forces that drove him – the pressure, the expectations, the need to generate higher returns, status, recognition – are the same ones that drive other rogue traders. Rogue trading activities, as Citron so aptly demonstrates, are not relegated to the Financial District in Manhattan.

What is frightening to consider is the fact that those same conditions that drove Citron to do what he did are still thriving across the country today, in every level of government. They're alive and well in small towns across the country, any place were an individual is expected to make something out of nothing. Elected officials are forced to make promises that they can't possibly keep if they get elected, and oftentimes those promises involve lower taxes and increased government services. That combination is as impossibly unsustainable today as it was in 1994. If anything, it's even more so today.

The simple lesson to take from this story is that you don't get something for nothing. There's always a cost or a risk involved. If you expect government services, you're going to have to pay for them, no matter what a politician asking for your vote tells you.

TOSHIHIDE IGUCHI AND DAIWA BANK, 1995

In ancient Roman times, when the universe was seen as being in the hands of the various gods, Janus was the deity who oversaw the changes in the world. He was depicted as having two faces, one looking to the future and the other gazing back into the past. With this dual-tined vision, Janus could simultaneously keep an eye on what was ahead, while simultaneously learning from what had already happened. His designation as the god of transitions led to the name January being assigned to the first month of the year. He is, quite frankly, a model for the intelligent trader. Janus, by understanding both the events of the past with an eye on the future, would no doubt have excelled at trading.

The two-faced Janus was a celebrated figure in Roman culture, but it's in stark contrast with the modern English concept of being "two-faced." In our modern lexicon, someone that is referred to as two-faced is a hypocrite or an otherwise untrustworthy person. A two-faced person will say one thing to one person, while saying the exact opposite to another.

The Asian lexicon for face is completely different. Despite Chinese writer Lin Yutang's declaration that the term face "cannot be translated or defined," there are characteristics that can be explained. At its core, the word encompasses dignity, prestige, honor, and respect. It is directly linked to one's status and social standing; a man with face is respected by others; there's social prestige linked to the amount of face that he commands. It can be both lost and gained, maintained and enhanced. It is something to be fought for and can be presented as a gift. It is, to be sure, an abstract and intangible concept.

In general, there are two kinds of face in Asian culture, *mianzi* and *lian*. Both are highly valuable to an Asian. To lose *mianzi* is equivalent to a decline in self-esteem and personal authority. It is the equivalent to a child being told by his parents that he has disappointed them.

Lian is moral character and equates to loss of trust within society. It is the most significant form of face because losing it brings into question one's own moral decency. It is, for business-men in Asia, a cultural requirement to have an established *lian*. Unlike *mianzi*, *lian* cannot be acquired through social standing. It must be earned through adherence to established protocols.

The importance of face is derived from the concept of com-munality. Social harmony is a primary rule in Asian life, and for millennia, the importance of the individual is downplayed over that of the family or the larger group as a whole. There's an expec-tation that individuals will work to preserve the reputation and the well-being – the *lian* – of the community. This is, of course, a stark contrast to the Western concept of honor, which is based on individual accomplishments and personal pride.

In Western culture, there is a tendency to speak to others in a straightforward manner. Phrases like "tell it like is" or "give it to me straight" are common. The idea that a trader on Wall Street would worry about someone's feelings when dealing in the markets is alien. If a trader did something stupid and lost a lot of money, they're going to be criticized. In Asian cultures, criticizing someone publically is fundamentally wrong because the recipient will lose face, no matter how much money is lost on a trade.

The concept goes even further. Chinese and Japanese businessmen would certainly never openly criticize anyone – especially a co-worker – in public. Violating these tenets can have repercussions, too. Embarrassment is a fate worse than death and they will go to any length necessary to avoid it. The emotional pain resulting from loss of face can result in a life-long enemy or even lead to a suicide. For many Asians, in fact, making a mistake and hiding it can be acceptable because the mistake itself is immaterial. It is understood that the individual will act to save face.

In 1983, a Japanese trader named Toshihide Iguchi was confronted with saving face and how he dealt with the situation lasted twelve years and end up costing his employer an astronomical amount of money.

*　　*　　*

Toshihide Iguchi lacked many of the qualities commonly associated with a rogue trader. He was a good student, to be sure, but not educated in the hallowed halls of the Ivy League or renown as a Wall Street "Master of the Universe." He graduated from high school in Kobe, Japan, in 1969, and went to college at Southwest Missouri State University where he was just one of 54 foreigners in a 12,000-member student body. He majored in psychology and was a member of both the university gymnastics club and the cheerleading squad.

In his spare time, Iguchi played the guitar and sang folk songs at a local coffee house. One former professor recalled that he "was a little shy," and another described him as "an A and B student and a courteous young man." During college, he became an American citizen, fell in love with an American woman, and got married. After graduating in 1975, he took a job selling trucks at a Chevrolet dealership.

Then, through his father's business connections, Iguchi landed an interview at a Japanese bank with an office in New York. It was a dream come true for Iguchi; bank jobs in Japan are considered the second-most desirable form of employment behind a government job. He had no practical banking experience or applicable educational background, but he did have a unique qualification that they rarely found anywhere else: He was Japanese. Daiwa Bank was looking for an American-education Japanese employee to serve as a liaison between the Japanese and American employees at their new Trust Company. Though "the bank only hired me because my father had a business relationship with them," he later admitted. Regardless of how he got the job, however, he reported for his first day of work on January 6, 1976, at Daiwa Bank.

Daiwa Bank began its life as the Osaka Nomura Bank, which was founded by Tokushichi Nomura in May 1918 in Osaka, Japan. Nomura had been engaged in the securities business in Osaka and he noticed that the other Japanese banks were only trying to deal with the largest companies in the major industries. There was, in Nomura's mind, a huge opportunity to service the small- and mid-sized companies that were being ignored. His plan was simply "to supply funds to these small and medium-sized enterprises."

By 1926, the nascent bank had grown in size and its securities department was large enough to be separated from the rest of the bank. The new entity was to be called the Nomura Securities Company, Ltd., a firm that remains Nomura Securities today. As a result of the split, he also changed the name of the bank to the Nomura Bank, Ltd.

In the early twentieth century, the Japanese *zaibatsu* were in control of the financial and industrial businesses within the Empire of Japan. They were essentially family-owned conglomerates that, due to their behemoth size, wielded considerable influence across the country. A typical group owned several businesses – both financial and industrial – and the various components worked in concert to dominate specific areas of the economy. The financial businesses provided operating capital to the industries, which were all controlled by the family that owned the *zaibatsu*.

Following Japan's defeat in World War II and the ensuing occupation, the Americans distrusted the former Japanese industrial set up. As the American forces were overseeing the rebuilding of Japan, the *zaibatsu* had to go. And one of the casualties of was the Nomura conglomerate. In October of 1948, the Nomura Bank, Ltd. officially became the Daiwa Bank, Limited. Two years later, the bank opened an office in New York. Fourteen years after that, they launched a pension trust business to hold assets for pension funds. It became a lucrative market, and in 1965, the trust business was separated into its own trust company, becoming The Daiwa Bank Trust Company.

A trust company is, by definition, a business that acts as a trustee on behalf of either an individual or a corporation. The trust company holds money and securities on behalf of their clients in safekeeping accounts. The trustee often manages the investments, keeps records, and prepares accounting reports. In some cases, the trustee will even pay the day-to-day expenses and distribute income.

In the case of the Daiwa Bank Trust Company in New York, the bank acted primarily as a trustee for Japanese mutual and pension funds. When a Japanese mutual fund, for example, bought American stocks, Daiwa held the securities for them in the United States. Daiwa would take delivery of the stock certificates, hold them in their vault and when the stock was sold, Daiwa would then take the certificates out of the vault and deliver them to the designated bank.

It was into this world of trust – an ironic term if ever there was one – that Iguchi was thrown into that January morning. He was assigned to the custody department at Daiwa Bank Trust, the group charged with handling securities. When he arrived, there were only two other employees in the department, an American woman and Iguchi's Japanese boss. But given that they were only settling ten to twelve securities on any given day, there was barely enough work to keep the three of them occupied.

Iguchi loved the job and he threw himself into it completely. His workday was reflective of the hours his Japanese colleagues kept, coming in no later than 8:00 in the morning and staying through 9:00 at night. The long hours paid off quickly because, after a year on the job, Iguchi was tapped to replace his boss, who was reassigned to the loan department. In other words, a little more than a year after graduating from college and with only a brief stint as a truck sales-man on his resume, Iguchi was in charge of the custody department.

The workings of a custody department are reminiscent of an old-time bank vault where the physical certificates are housed. It was originally called the cashiers department and the employees were in charge of receiving and delivering the securities, and controlling the money from the securities' movements. Due to the presence of large quantities of valuable securities certificates, access was under-standably limited. And just like an old-time bank vault, the cashiers department was housed behind steel bars that looked like a maximum security prison. Those bars earned the area the nickname of "the cage."

Stock and bond certificates are documents that represent an individual's ownership of either shares of company stock or company debt. The physical certificate identifies the issuing company, the number of shares or bonds, and the registered owner of the certifi-cate. They also have a unique certificate number that is used to track the certificate once it's issued. In the 1970s, when Iguchi first started at Daiwa, stock certificate deliveries had to be made before 11:30 AM whenever someone sold a stock. The certificate would be delivered by messenger and the recipient would examine the certificate closely to make sure that all the details of the transaction were correct. Of particular importance was an assurance that the certificate had not been forged. After receipt, the receiving bank would issue a check that was picked up by messenger after 1:00 in the afternoon, who would then run the check back to the bank that had sold the stock.

It probably goes without saying that the entire process was wildly cumbersome and inefficient. By the mid-1970s, the entirety of Wall Street – brokers, securities dealers, and banks – came together to make the process more efficient. The result was the creation of a centralized clearing authority, what is today called the Depository Trust Company (DTC). It was a major advance in terms of the speed with which securities transactions are cleared.

DTC, as its name suggests, is a trust company, and is the most widely used U.S. securities depository. Most U.S. equities and corporate bonds are transferred through DTC, and DTC members deposit all of their stock and bond certificates with the company. Certificates are simply moved from one account within the DTC to another as needed, as opposed to sending them via messenger to other banks. Everything is self-contained within the company, and there is no need for physical movement or re-registration when they change hands. No more sending messengers with certificates from location to location all day long. Ownership changes hands via book-entry, meaning that their movement is recorded within an electronic record keeping system.

By 1979, as far as Iguchi was concerned, his business was booming. He had three clerks working for him and together they were settling upwards of fifty trades a day. Just two years later, Daiwa became the largest manager of pension trusts in Japan. Iguchi's importance skyrocketed and his custody department accounted for 50% of Daiwa's profits in the New York office.

He was, in a nutshell, living the embodiment of the American Dream. He'd worked hard to get where he was – by now, staying at the office until 11:00 every night – and everything was falling into place. He had a beautiful home in the suburb of Kinnelon, New

Jersey, and a wife whom he loved very much. Two children rounded out the picture-perfect family for the Christmas cards and a good job at a major bank to help pay for it all. He took few vacations and spent most of his time at work – one neighbor even mentioned, "I've never seen him, and we live right across the street" – but that was just his nature. Iguchi had face, and that's all that really mattered.

*　　*　　*

By 1982, Iguchi's responsibilities had expanded beyond simply running the custody department to include investing Daiwa Trust's excess capital, which he did by purchasing floating rate notes (FRN). FRNs are bonds with interest rates that float off an index, most often LIBOR. The bonds' interest rate resets on a schedule that depends on the particular bond, but usually resets monthly, quarterly, semi-annually, or annually. They are considered a relatively safe investment because they're not susceptible to very much interest rate risk. If interest rates move unexpectedly, the investor knows that any storm can be weathered until the next reset period. As a result of the floating interest rates, the prices of FRNs don't move very much either.

There is an employment practice that is particular to Japan: the concept of Japanese home-staff. Japanese employees are expected to spend their entire working career at the bank, moving around from department to department and location to location. A typical Japanese bank employee works on these rotating assignments, with each rotation lasting anywhere from three to five years. There is typically little prior notice for the employee regarding when he'll be transferred or where he'll end up. The result generates a great deal of anxiety over an employee's next assignment. A bad assignment could set back one's career for years, whereas a good assignment could vault them ahead.

This practice often leads to those with hiring authority looking out for their friends. For example, Japanese employees who went the same school will often help others in their group through favorable assignments. It is, of course, a quid-pro-quo arrangement. The beneficiary of the favor is indebted to his colleague and is obliged to return a favor in the future.

I had a personal experience with this practice when I worked at the Bank of Tokyo in New York in the 1990s. There was a particular young Japanese home-staffer in the office that had been in New York for about three years. He was anxiously awaiting the news of his next assignment. New York, I learned, was considered a great assignment, because the employee received housing that was paid for by the bank, the work hours weren't nearly as grueling as they were in Japan, and many of them grew very fond of the New York City nightlife. Of course, I had to take that with a grain of salt because, as someone who was from the New York area, being told that it wasn't a great place could potentially cause me to lose face.

The young man finally learned of his new assignment: He was to be transferred to the Human Resources department in Tokyo. I initially felt badly for him. It's not that I have anything against HR, but compared to the world of buying and selling bonds, it seemed like a demotion. He was a hard worker who had done well in New York, so I couldn't understand exactly why he was being punished.

But he was ecstatic with the news. As it turned out, in the Japanese mindset, moving to HR was a huge promotion. I asked another Japanese employee about it and he explained that being transferred to HR was a compliment. As an HR employee, he would help decide where other home-staff employees would be assigned, which means that he'd be in the position to do favors for his friends and his group. Because the home-staff are life-long employees, an HR assignment meant he'd have plenty of years in the future to cash in on those favors. Of course, it also means he can stick any enemies in less-than-desirable position too.

Daiwa Bank had one such Japanese home-staff named Yamada, who was part of a new department trading U.S. Treasury bonds and using Daiwa's own capital. By the end of 1983, this home-staff trader was producing a staggering 80% of the profit for the entire Daiwa office in New York. He was the quintessential rock star trader, at least in the eyes of his Japanese coworkers.

After hearing about Yamada's amazing results, the General Manager of the Trust office, a man by the name of Mr. Ueba, approached Iguchi, telling him that he should be able to do as well for the Trust Company as Yamada was doing for the Bank. It was, in the most basic sense, a challenge to Iguchi. Ueba was turning making money into a competition between the Trust Company and the Bank.

However, Iguchi would have to operate with some parameters. He had to limit his trading to only $10 million at any time and he would only be allowed to trade FRNs. With that, Iguchi was off and running as the official bond trader of Daiwa Trust, while still maintaining his duties of overseeing the custody department.

He dove in head-first, buying and selling FRNs. He was, interestingly enough, settling his own trades, so there was nobody looking over his shoulder to make sure he was playing by the rules. "No one questioned who should settle proprietary trades," Iguchi would later say. "There was not a scintilla of concern about letting the head of the securities custody department engage in both proprietary trading and settlement."

By March of 1983, Iguchi had made approximately $50,000 trading FRNs, which was an exceptional return. That month, Salomon Brothers began underwriting a new FRN that they promised would trade well in the secondary market, assuring Iguchi he'd make a profit if he bought the issue. He was told that the price would jump above 99.00 as soon as the FRN "broke the syndicate." That's a way of saying that once the investment banking syndicate that underwrote the securities had dissolved, the price would soar. Typically the syndicates break up when they've sold all of the securities in the issue. After the break-up, there are no longer price restrictions on secondary sales of the securities.

Iguchi jumped at the offer and bought $10 million of the bond and it immediately dropped in price. He gave Salomon an order to buy it back, but they told him too many of their customers were also trying to sell. The salesman said, "My trader says you should wait until April because right now, he is trying to get rid of his own unsold inventory."

Iguchi became irate and he felt that he'd been suckered. "I bought it for a flip, not a keep!" he screamed into the phone at the salesman. A few days later, Iguchi sold the FRN back to Salomon for a price of 98.10, losing a total of $70,000 on the trade. Although it wasn't a monumental loss, it was still a loss. And it was big enough to have wiped out his entire profit for the year, plus an extra $20,000 thrown in for good measure.

While most Western traders might take a loss in stride, Iguchi was crestfallen. "I could imagine the disappointed face of Mr. Ueba," he said. "Without a doubt, he would reprimand me." Again, stern talking from a manager is not something traders are immune to and most traders on Wall Street have been on the wrong end of that conversation more than once. It's just part of the job. You win some, you lose some and hopefully you win more than you lose. When you win, you get a bigger bonus. When you lose, you get taken to the woodshed. Either way, you're usually still employed the next day.

But Iguchi was not a typical American trader. He was a Japanese trader who carried with him the extensive cultural baggage that had been heaped on him since his earliest days. This situation and the accompanying disappointment of his boss weren't about losing money. It was a matter of losing face, something that he could not live with. A string of promotions had elevated him to an accomplished position at the bank, but a loss of face would stay with him forever, a scar he would carry throughout his career. So he decided to hide the loss. As he would later admit, "I decided to compromise my integrity to save my future."

*   *   *

Iguchi's plan was naturally to make back the loss through trading. The problem he was up against, though, was the fact that FRNs aren't the best trading instrument around, as their prices don't move very much. In other words, buying low and selling high isn't so lucrative in the FRN market. FRNs are considered a conservative investment. They'll make a safe return in the long run, but the returns are neither speedy nor massive.

U.S. Treasury bonds, however, will fluctuate in price a bit more, and Iguchi reasoned that it was easier to make the money back in the Treasury bond market. At the time, the U.S. was riding a bull bond market and prices had been rising since early 1982. They just seemed to keep going up, so Iguchi figured it would be easy to make the money back before anybody realized it was missing.

His first order went to his salesman at Paine Webber. It was a buy order for $10 million of the 30-Year U.S. Treasury. He bought the bond at a price of 98-24, which is the way bond prices are quoted. The price is quoted in 32nds of a point, so a 98-24 price means 98 and 24/32. Because the 30-Year is the longest maturity bond, it's often called "the long bond," or sometimes just "the bond."

In what seemed to be a sad pattern for Iguchi, however, his purchase was followed by an immediate drop in the market. He then sold the position on the advice of his salesman just a few hours later: "I think you should cut the loss and take a look at it again later," he told Iguchi. Iguchi took the advice and unloaded his holdings, by then the price had dropped to 97-24. In the space of a few hours, Iguchi had lost another $100,000. His total loss had now grown to $170,000. "I went into the bathroom," Iguchi recalled moments after the disastrous trade, "and no one was there. I saw my image in the mirror. It did not look familiar."

The following day, Iguchi processed the transaction himself and sent out the money out to Paine Webber. At this point, he was the only one in the office who knew the full extent of his losses. He didn't account for the missing funds in the books that day; he'd worry about that later. For now, he had bigger issues. He needed to make back even more money.

At this point, getting caught potentially meant getting fired. But if nobody found out about it, he reasoned, he could keep his job, not to mention save face. Every time he made a trade going forward – something he had to do with increasing frequency – he needed to keep it a secret. He devised a way to keep the trade confirmations out of sight of his coworkers: "Each time I bought or sold bonds, the dealer sent a confirmation ticket to the bank by mail. They were delivered to me, and I kept them in my drawer where no one would see." It wasn't the most high-tech method of deception, but it worked. The only catch was that he maintained two piles of trade confirmations: one of off-the-books trades that were aimed at recouping his losses, and one of on-the-books that were part of his daily work. As long as he kept the two separate, he thought he just might just get away with it.

He quickly realized that buying and selling $10 million worth of bonds each time wasn't going to make back the money he needed, so he doubled the size of his trades to $20 million. It was run-of-the-mill gambler logic. If I can make money by betting a certain amount, I can make twice as much by betting double. Mathematically, it makes sense. But the rules of math aren't flexible as the knife cuts both ways. Anytime you've got the potential to make twice as much, you can also lose twice as much. Unfortunately for Iguchi, the latter was his reality. He was soon carrying $420,000 in losses.

Around the middle of 1983, Iguchi's loss had ballooned to $700,000 and his salesman at Salomon Brothers mentioned that the sales manager wanted to meet Iguchi and his boss, Mr. Ueba, at their office. Before Iguchi had time to think, the salesman told him that the sales manager was already on his way. Iguchi immediately went into full-blown panic mode. This was it. The Salomon sales manager was going to tell Ueba about Iguchi's trades. It wouldn't be long before Iguchi was fired. What's more, an outsider bringing to light Iguchi's impropriety was an even greater embarrassment in Japanese culture than simple personal failure. Not only a loss of face for Iguchi, but for Daiwa Trust as a whole. It was a tidal wave of destruction for Iguchi.

The meeting lasted ten minutes and Iguchi didn't even know it had actually started. He was still sitting at his desk when Ueba materialized in front of him. "Iguchi-kun," he addressed the trader. "I just had a long talk with a sales manager from Salomon Brothers." Iguchi braced himself. "He said you were a very good trader. Keep it up!"

And that was that. Rather than delivering a condemnation paired with a pink slip, Ueba had come down to praise Iguchi. Anyone familiar with Salomon Brothers in the 1980s, however, would immediately recognize the situation. The firm was notorious for looking at their customers as cows who needed to be milked on a regular basis. Any customer who lost hundreds of thousands of dollars every time they traded was considered a great customer. By the end of that year, based in part on Salomon's endorsement, Iguchi was promoted to Assistant Vice President.

Making Iguchi's losses all the more personally embarrassing was the fact that his counterpart at Daiwa Bank, Yamada, was continuing to show amazing returns. In fact, by year-end 1983, Yamada had booked several million dollars in profits. While others were quick to praise Yamada's talents, Iguchi became suspicious. His own shortcomings notwithstanding, he didn't see how it was possible for anyone – regardless of talent – to make such profit saddled with the $3 million trading limit.

One day when Iguchi was speaking with his salesman from First Boston, the truth suddenly erupted. The salesman asked Iguchi about his $39 million position, then quickly backtracked when he realized it was the position of Daiwa Bank and not Daiwa Trust. Suddenly it was clear how Yamada was making such exorbitant profits: He, too, was engaging in unauthorized trading that far exceeding his trading limits. "How bizarre was it that two U.S.-educated Japanese officers operating independently ended up in the same situation?" he asked rhetorically.

Yamada ended up leaving the bank in March of 1985 to begin working as a trader at an American investment bank. Iguchi said of the departure, "I was more puzzled than envious." His suspicion was supported by the fact that Japanese home-staff employees rarely left the company they worked for. Again, they saw their jobs as employ-ment-for-life. Officially, Yamada reported a trading profit of $4 million in 1984, but Iguchi was convinced that the numbers had been doctored. He believed that management had discovered the fraud and, rather than disgracing Yamada and Daiwa Bank with the loss, they allowed him to leave for another job. "The only possible reason I could think of was that management let him go with an understand-ing that he kept his mouth shut," Iguchi said of Yamada's departure.

* * *

As the old saying goes, April showers bring May flowers. In April of 1984, many towns along a thirty-mile stretch or the Passaic River in New Jersey discovered that that those April showers brought massive flooding. During the first week of April, that area received a record amount of rain, turning Kinnelon, New Jersey, and other towns nearby into veritable islands that were only accessible by boat. It was called the worst flood to hit the area in 80 years and damages exceeded $330 million.

Iguchi woke that morning at 6:00 AM to discover that his house was completely flooded. Most people would have call into their office and explain the situation and taken the day off. But Iguchi didn't have that luxury. He had recently financed a $150 million Treasury position in the repo market and the financing ended that day. When he woke up in the morning, his first thought wasn't about the flooding. It was about getting to the office early so that he could book a new repo trade to continue to finance the position. In short, it was absolutely vital that he made it into work – or at least to a phone – so he could call someone to book the new trade.

The flood had knocked out both the electricity and the phone lines, and remember, this was before the days of cellular phones. Looking out of his window, he could see that his entire neighborhood was flooded. Water was everywhere. The street in front of his house was feet-deep in water and it extended across his neighbors' houses. If he couldn't book a new repo trade, his counterparty would call the bank and ask what they should do with the trade rolling-off. Given that the trade was unauthorized, it wouldn't take long for senior officers at the bank to get involved.

It then occurred to him that his train station was well above street level, meaning it was out of the reach of the flood waters.

And as an added bonus, there were payphones there. All he had to do was get to the station and take the next train or book a new repo trade over the phone. But the station was two miles away. And the difficulty was compounded by the fact that the neighborhood was entirely underwater. Desperate times call for desperate measures, so Iguchi got dressed and began making his way to the station. He had barely reached the street before he realized that this was an impossible task. The water was just too deep for him to wade through, so he feared he'd never make the call on time.

Just when he was about to give up, he remembered that his sons had a small plastic boat that they used for the family swimming pool. It was usually left in the backyard and just might be what he was looking for. Iguchi lurched back to his house and found the boat floating there. "I plowed through the murky water and found the plastic oar still attached," he recalled, "so I climbed in and began rowing."

It must have looked like an old comedy skit. There sat Iguchi, an Assistant Vice President at Daiwa Trust, furiously rowing a child's plastic boat down the middle of a flooded street, past his neighbors' houses and on to the train station. He paddled all the way and when he arrived at the station, he learned that the trains weren't running. But the payphones still worked. He quickly called his counterparty and extended the repo trade for one more day. His salvation had been delivered to him by way of a plastic boat. "I was relieved that disaster had been avoided," he said. "I rowed back home wondering how much longer I could continue juggling."

This event took Iguchi to a whole new level of complexity and nefariousness. He realized that at some point he had to account for the money he'd lost over the past year. He couldn't just keep hiding the losses by borrowing money in the repo market. Aside from the constant worry of discovery at the office, some similar event could easily expose his entire fraud.

Earlier in 1984, a Daiwa Trust customer had purchased $10 million of a U.S. Treasury bond and they arranged for Daiwa to hold the securities in their custody account. In other words, Iguchi himself was essentially holding it. When Iguchi saw that $10 million arrive in the customer's account, it was like a lightning bolt hitting him. "I saw this and an idea flashed in my head: I could borrow their T-notes to raise money," he said. He was going to borrow the customer's Treasurys to raise cash to cover his own losses.

Taking customer property, even to the most innocent financial mind, is an illegal act. The reason securities are held in a custody account – segregated from the bank's own money – is because they belong to the customer; they're customer property. Even temporarily "borrowing" the securities is equivalent of stealing from the customer. And it's beyond illegal. "The only hitch would come when they were ready to sell [the bonds]," Iguchi said. "Then I would have to get them back to make delivery." He wasn't focused on the future, he was too concerned with covering his immediate losses. If the issue came back, he'd deal with it then.

Something that was working in his favor was the lack of technology in the financial industry. "In those days, when we didn't have computers, we manually jotted down the balance of each issue from the record book and typed a report," Iguchi said of the firm's accounting methods. That meant it was relatively easy for him to hide the Treasury bonds. All he had to do was record the position in their record books, and Voila, the bonds magically appeared in the customer's account.

The customer's Treasury bond purchase was the beginning of a trend for Japanese investors, who began building-up major U.S. Treasury positions in the mid-1980s. In fact, by 1985, Japanese investors were buying almost half of all new U.S. Treasurys that were being issued. Daiwa Securities was considered one of the "Big Four" Japanese brokerage houses involved, along with Nomura,

Nikko, and Yamaichi. By 1985, Daiwa was holding over $700 million in U.S. Treasurys for Japanese customers, which provided Iguchi with plenty of bonds to "borrow" so he could hide his losses. It was a lucky break for Iguchi. As he himself admitted, "Had it not been for the phenomenal surge of investment in U.S. T-notes by our Japanese customers, I would have been forced to give up."

If Iguchi was a gambler, suffice it to say that Lady Luck did not smile on him. By the summer of 1984, his loss – which had started as $70,000 – had grown to over $20 million. Within a year, that number was at $30 million. The uphill climb he'd begun a few years earlier was now turning into a full-blown mountain.

Technology finally came to Daiwa in 1986. By February of that year, the custody department was fully computerized, though Iguchi was still resisting modernization for obvious reasons. It would, to be sure, make hiding his losses much harder. But there was a saving grace in the technological revolution: Reconciliation of the clearing accounts holding Treasuries was still done manually. It was another in a long series of temporary reprieves that prolonged his run as a rogue trader. In September of that year, another Heaven-sent bonus landed in his lap. Daiwa's New York branch officially moved out of the Financial District to Midtown Manhattan, but still left Iguchi and his custody department in their old downtown building. The geographic separation from senior executives gave him a little more breathing room to continue his activities.

At the time, the custody department had grown significantly from Iguchi's early days. They were holding north of $3 billion in stocks and bonds for their Japanese clients, up from only $20 million when Iguchi started at the bank. Iguchi's own trading positions had followed a similar trajectory. His profit/loss numbers had swings of as much as $30 million at a time as he whipped around Treasury bond positions as large as $300 million. It was ironic that the top Wall Street banks knew Iguchi was trading hundreds of millions of Treasurys from his tiny downtown office, whereas nobody else at his own bank seemed to have any idea.

But bad trading luck continued to follow him; it seemed that no what he did, he couldn't win. When the market went in his direction, he held on to the positions too long. Inevitably, the market would turn and his gains disintegrated into thin air. Alternatively, when the market moved against him, he would leave orders to limit his losses, only to see the market rebound after he'd sold at a loss.

As his losses grew, Iguchi was forced to rely on selling more and more customer-owned bonds. That problem was compounded by the fact that those bonds paid coupons to the owners. In the case of a U.S. Treasury bond, it pays interest every six months based on its coupon amount. Given that he'd sold $30 million worth of customer-owned bonds by this point, he needed to come up with about $1.5 million every six months just to make those coupon payments.

To make the payments, he did the only thing he could do, namely sell more customer-owned bonds. It was a classic Ponzi scheme, where he would steal from one group to pay back another group from whom he'd already stole. The scheme is named for Charles Ponzi, an Italian-American businessman who conned investors out of nearly $20 million in the 1920s, an astronomically high sum of money for the time. Iguchi was paying out about $3 million a year to carry his loss, and it was building on itself like a snake eating its own tail. At this point, in his mind, the only way out of his hole was to pull off a massive trade.

*   *   *

In January of 1987, Iguchi tried one more gambler's trick to save himself. He decided that he was in too deep to just make a few million dollars at a time on a winning trade. He was physically and mentally exhausted and he didn't know how much longer he could keep it up. It was now or never, in his mind, and he needed to make it all back on a single trade.

He called eight different banks and bought $125 million in bonds from each one, for a total of $1 billion. His plan was to let it ride and cross his fingers. To call it a mammoth trade doesn't do it justice. To put this in perspective, every one-point move in the market would represent 1% of the entire position, or $10 million. And in the late 1980s when interest rates moved around considerably, a one-point move in a single day wasn't uncommon.

Something Iguchi either didn't know or didn't appreciate was the fact that the traders at the banks talked to each other, and word soon spread that he was holding a billion dollar position. As soon as he'd completed his buying spree, the market moved up a full point, making him $10 million without even thinking about it. The problem was, however, it was only a mark-to-market gain. In other words, it was a gain only on paper. For him to realize that profit, he'd have to sell the position.

So he held onto his long position of $1 billion for almost a full month, watching the market move in his favor most of the time. On any given day, his mark-to-market profit was between $10 and $20 million. But just when it looked like he'd make it out alive, the market got stuck and refused to move any higher. Beginning that spring, the stock market started a relentless climb, which pushed the bond market lower. Iguchi's monster position began to move against him. Fear began to grip him as he watched the position go from a $20 million profit to a $30 million loss to a $50 million loss. When he finally threw in the towel and admitted defeat, his one-time profit of $20 million had become an $80 million loss. It was a loss of face that would be next to impossible for the once-proud man to overcome. But he figured that he'd come this far, and there was no way to go but forward. His pride – his face – wouldn't let him publicly admit the magnitude of his defeat.

*   *   *

In 1988, Iguchi got a new boss, a man named Kenji Yasui, who became the head of all of Daiwa's North America operations. The day Yasui arrived in New York, he walked directly to Iguchi's desk and said, "I've heard a lot about you." The two exchanged pleasantries, and then Yasui got to the point: "Would it be possible for you to move up to the Midtown office and start a T-bond trading team?"

In other words, Iguchi was once again being promoted after sustaining monumental losses. The man, whose career had started at a Chevrolet truck dealership, was being asked if he wanted to be the head of Daiwa's bond trading operation. It would be a dream come true for any bond trader on Wall Street, and no one in their right mind would turn it down. But Iguchi wasn't necessarily in his right mind and he knew he couldn't keep covering his losses if he was no longer in charge of custody. So he declined the promotion, saying "No. I'm afraid not, because this custody department will not function without me." It was, most likely, not the response that Yasui was expecting, but he took it in stride. "I see," Yasui replied, "Then could you train another trader here?"

Iguchi agreed to train the other trader, a man named Mr. Masuda, who was being transferred to New York from the Tokyo office. The request wasn't an accident. As it turned out, Masuda was brought to New York to take care of a trading loss – this one known to senior officials – that had been accumulated years earlier. Back in 1984, Yamada – the man whom Iguchi was originally pitted against to generate trading profits – had lost approximately $30 million, and Mr. Yasui was the point man charged with making back that loss.

So here stood the man who had masterminded the cover-up of a massive trading loss, asking a trader who he thought was the pinnacle of trading success to assist him in recouping the losses. The catch was that the loss was no longer $30 million. Back in Tokyo, Yasui had spearheaded a team that had tried to trade their way back to profitability. Those trades had gone against them, sinking Yamada's original loss to $100 million. By now, they'd abandoned those attempts and decided to go with Plan B. Masuda – after being trained by the brilliant mind of Iguchi – would be their Plan B.

On one hand, it's mind-boggling to consider that there were two groups within the same organization trying desperately to make back trading losses. On the other hand, though, it's not surprising, given the value the Japanese place on saving face. According to Iguchi, "Unfortunately, it was a part of our corporate culture to take care of any problem on our own. This was a show responsibility as much as a reluctance to admit a mistake." In other words, saving face trumped everything else.

To complement his efforts, Iguchi was assigned two young home-staffers to supplement his trading operation: Araki and Yagi. Araki was charged with buying and selling Treasury bonds, whereas Yagi was trading U.S. Treasury bond futures contracts. Both had individual trading limits of $50 million and the desk had a collective loss limit of $1 million. Within three months, both young men had suffered losses of $500,000 each, which meant the desk had reached its loss limit and the pair stopped trading. In April, they were allowed to resume again, in the hopes they could make it all back.

But just as those April showers bring May flowers, April is also the cruelest month. By the end of the month, the pair had sunk even further to a $3 million collective loss. Iguchi willingly turned a blind eye, letting them continue. They adding to their positions, repeating all of the same mistakes as Iguchi admitted that the team was "breaking all the rules of trading, such as never add to a losing position and don't marry your position." Soon enough, they had amassed a $15 million loss.

While the U.S. bond market continued to torture Iguchi, the Japanese stock market was surging. The Nikkei average reached 38,915 on December 29, 1989, and there was rampant speculation in Japanese real estate. Many commentators predicted that Japan was poised to take over the world, economically speaking. The world had seemingly bought in to the idea that there were never-ending profits in Japan. As a result, Daiwa had an unrealized profit of $13 billion on its vast stock portfolio.

By contrast, Iguchi himself was carrying a $565 million loss. He rationalized that the bank could easily absorb his loss; all they needed to do was sell of a small portion of their stock holdings. In his mind, he began planning his confession. He'd fall on his sword, in true Japanese fashion, and admit his mistakes. It would cost him dearly, but at least he could finally rid himself of the huge weight he'd been carrying. Just one little piece of the Daiwa stock portfolio. It would be as easy as extracting a splinter.

But that wouldn't last as an option. In the subsequent months, the Nikkei began a slow retreat. Within a year, the bank's $13 billion profit was whittled down to a paltry $3 billion and completely disappeared just two years later. And Iguchi's losses continued to grow. In 1990, both of Iguchi's protégés' trading losses were up to $350 million. Iguchi agreed to take over the losses after they were transferred back to Japan following their home-staff stint in New York; he bid them farewell by saying, "Don't worry about anything." In a moment of what can only be described as a morally ambiguous demonstration of personal character, he took their illegal activities upon himself, allowing them to climb up the Japanese corporate ladder without a blemish on their careers.

Yasui, too, left the New York office and returned to Japan, replaced as General Manager by a man named Hiroshi Ikeda. In April of 1991, Ikeda received what should have been a disturbing phone call from the Daiwa headquarters in Tokyo. They'd heard a rumor from an unknown source that the Daiwa office in New York was carrying a $100 million trading loss. Ikeda ignored the news and simply "brushed it off as a bad joke." The Federal Reserve, however, heard the same rumor and sent an examiner over to the Daiwa offices.

Iguchi, for obvious reasons, didn't find the rumor so easy to ignore, "It scared me that people outside the bank had a better idea of what was really going on," he said. In what can only be called a catastrophic failure of the regulatory agency, the Fed was unable to discover any irregularities, and they relegated the rumor to being the same bad joke that Ikeda thought it was.

But the problems with the Federal Reserve didn't stop there. As it turned out, Iguchi wasn't the only one carrying a deep, dark secret. His employer had one of its own. The firm's remnant downtown trading room was still located in the World Financial Center, next to the site of the World Trade Center in downtown New York City. The problem, which might seem trivial, was that they'd never told their Japanese regulators they had a second trading room. As such, they couldn't mention it in any of their U.S. regulatory filings, because doing so would let the Japanese regulators know that it existed. And that revelation would open yet another can of metaphorical worms.

As Iguchi explained, "Well, we are, in fact, misleading the Fed, but the true motive is to conceal the downtown trading operation from the [Japanese Ministry of Finance], not the Fed." They had let their star trader maintain his offices downtown, but once they had concealed its existence from the Ministry of Finance, there was no turning back. From the moment they'd decided to keep that second trading room hidden, Daiwa executives had taken their first steps down a dark – and illegal – path, and they had to continue to keep the secret rather than admit that they'd deceived authorities. By doing so, Daiwa officials could preserve their own company face. "Perhaps Yasui was more concerned about the Daiwa Trust problem getting dredged up than I had realized," Iguchi later said of the secrecy.

The firm's method of disguising the operation was relatively simple. Whenever the Fed scheduled an audit, company personnel scrambled to modify the appearance of the downtown trading room. Cardboard boxes were brought in, along with an assortment of random items, and everything was stacked willy-nilly throughout the room, making it look like a non-descript storage area. "We disguised the trading room to look like a storage room by piling up cardboard boxes on our desks, stacking a ladder, buckets, and whatever we could find on the floor," Iguchi explained. Once the audits were over, the items were removed and the office was returned to its original condition as a trading operation.

But the secret was a potential problem, and a major problem at that, both for Iguchi and for Daiwa. If Daiwa admitted to the Fed that they had been concealing something, they could expect to receive a lengthy and thorough audit from the Fed. That would be a problem because an extensive audit could reveal the Yamada loss from years before. So the decision was made to conceal it, at least for as long as they could. At the same time, Iguchi's losses had now grown to an amount in excess of $800 million.

*   *   *

As 1995 dawned, Daiwa Bank was continuing its original business of providing loans to small and mid-sized businesses. They'd expanded their custody services beyond pension trusts to include holding securities, real estate, and private banking. The Daiwa

Bank Group – which included both Daiwa Bank and Daiwa Trust – still operated primarily in Japan and had assets of approximately $197 billion, making them one of the largest banks in the world. But change was coming, and not in a good way.

The custody department was missing more than half a billion dollars' worth of securities; the Treasury bonds that Iguchi had sold in order to cover his losses. Approximately $377 million of U.S. Treasuries that belonged to Daiwa customers were gone, as was $134 million that belonged to Daiwa itself. Iguchi's loss had swollen to unimaginable proportions. The trader had amassed a deficit of more than $950 million, an amount that was in excess of 13,500 times the original loss of $70,000 he sustained thirteen years earlier. He had been carrying that ever-growing loss, not to mention the stress that accompanied it, for more than a decade. Taken as a whole, it's incomprehensible. But for Iguchi, it was all too real. And things were about to get even more real.

In July of 1995, Toshihide Iguchi decided that he could no longer continue carrying around the burden of his secret. It was time for him to admit his errors and take ownership of his actions. The reasons he gave for his confession hinged on his family: "I had two teenage sons whom I loved, and to me nothing was more important than keeping their respect. My mind was set in regaining my dignity for my loved ones. I had caused enough damage."

Beginning on July 21, he would draft a total of five confessional letters over the course of the next two months. In those letters, he would work to convince his superiors to hide the losses and not report him. He was counting on them being steeped in the same Japanese tradition that he was. Specifically, he was hoping they would subscribe to the belief that the group was more important than the individual, and they would prefer to save the collective face of Daiwa Trust. As it turned out, his hopes were well founded, as bank officials were happy to work with him. They wanted to save face as badly as he did.

In his first letter, Iguchi laid out the details of what he'd done in a 30-page document stamped "Personal and Confidential" and addressed to Mr. Fujita, the CEO of Daiwa Bank. After introducing himself as "Toshihide Iguchi of the New York Branch," Iguchi went on to confess his losses for thirteen years. After his initially contrite words, however, his tone turned conspiratorial. He reminded the CEO of what he called "the big accident" that had been concealed in the past. It was a thinly-veiled reference to the losses sustained by Yamada and how the firm had worked to cover it up. Tying in his own fraud, he said, "If this problem becomes known to the U.S. regulatory authorities, our U.S. operations will be jeopardized. Furthermore, the Ministry of Finance will also receive strong criticism for their lax oversight."

Iguchi's chutzpah was nearly as grand as his losses. In no uncertain terms, he was putting the entire reputation of the Japanese Ministry of Finance – along with the well-being of Daiwa's U.S. operations – in the hands of the CEO. He was essentially deflecting the wrath of his superiors by saying that if his own illegal actions became public, a major Japanese governmental agency would be publicly embarrassed. It would be a humiliation for the entire nation. But Fujita had the power to prevent that national catastrophe. All they had to do was keep it a secret. He warned of the dire consequences if the matter was not handled solely by Japanese authorities, as no other agency anywhere in the world – especially not in the United States – would understand the importance of saving face. "No one else has any knowledge about it," Iguchi wrote of the situation, "and until we are ready to disclose it, all will be business as usual."

Fortunately for all involved, Iguchi also had a plan to unwind the mess. Now that the situation was out in the open, Daiwa could go into the bond market, buy back the missing securities and place them in the customer accounts. That would cover the theft of customer property, which would erase any regulatory issue within the U.S. Then, there would be no need for the involvement of the U.S. authorities and the matter could be resolved internally.

Finally, all the bank had to do next was to take the trading loss. It would be a momentary embarrassment, but would eventually fade into the fog of distant memory. The bank would save face, while at the same time avoiding the humiliation caused by the discovery of the cover-up by U.S. regulatory authorities. All-in-all, from Iguchi's perspective, it wasn't such a bad plan.

After he'd sent the letter, one can only imagine the anxiety going through his mind as he waited for a reply. He waited a few of days with no news and then began to fear that his letter hadn't been received. So he wrote a second letter on July 23, which he stapled to a copy of the original letter. In the second letter, Iguchi expressed concern that his first letter had not been received, and went on to again reassure the CEO that there was no possibility of detection by U.S. authorities if Daiwa followed Iguchi's plan. "To make this incident our own domestic problem, all we have to do is buy back the missing U.S. Treasury bonds," he wrote. "Not even internal auditors will notice any irregularities."

The next day, Iguchi received a phone call from Kenji Yasui in the Tokyo office. Yasui was the man put in charge of covering up Yamada's loss, so he and Iguchi were kindred spirits of sorts. Iguchi immediately pledged to "do anything I can to help the bank," and Yasui told him that they needed to buy back the Treasurys that were missing from clients' accounts. "Once that's done," Iguchi replied, "the New York branch will be made whole, and we can take care of this problem in Japan." The conspiracy was now in effect.

The next day, Iguchi penned a third letter. In it, he warned Fujita and Yasui of the dangers associated with manipulating the books of the Daiwa offices in New York. In doing so, the firm was making itself vulnerable to a U.S. investigation, because it would be a violation of federal laws in the United States.

Following receipt of that letter, the Tokyo office put a plan in place a plan to protect everyone. Masahiro Tsuda, the General Manager of the New York office, was notified and informed of what had happened. He called a meeting on July 29 with a few top officials, as well as Iguchi. The team met in a hotel room away from the Daiwa office, so that no one would sense that there was anything wrong. At the meeting, Tsuda informed Iguchi, "From now on, we are in this together. Your secret is at the corporate level, so don't hold anything back."

Mentioning Iguchi's "secret" was no doubt a great relief to the trader, as he could be reassured that the firm wasn't planning on holding him as the public scapegoat. That was not to say there wouldn't be professional consequences, but so long as he wasn't going to be the public image of an egregious embarrassment, he could recover. Tsuda also told him that the bank planned to report the incident to the Ministry of Finance after the firm's semi-annual earnings report was released in November, which indicated to Iguchi that the bank intended to keep the matter within the relatively safe cultural confines of Japanese regulatory authorities.

Immediately following, Iguchi wrote a fourth letter. Following the instructions he'd received from Tsuda to not "hold anything back." He provided detailed accounts of the initial loss, the lengths he went through to cover it up, the losses that followed, including from the sale of customer assets. He explained, too, his methodology for forging account records.

After reading the letter, Daiwa management took the extraordinary step of authorizing Iguchi to continue selling customer securities in order to meet coupon payments. In other words, they were approving the Ponzi scheme he'd implemented years earlier. It would later come to light that this decision was not a unanimous one.

As there is in every office environment, Daiwa was rife with inter-office politics. The domestic division of the bank saw the international division as their fierce rivals, despite the fact that they worked for the same organization. As a result, the domestic division officials thought the firm should fully disclose the incident immediately. They saw it as an opportunity to disgrace the international division and thereby cause the group to lose face. The domestic team felt they might gain more control over the company and then have access to the top managerial spots.

The international division, however, lobbied to keep the secret, citing the scandalous nature of the fraud that would forever tarnish Daiwa's reputation. In the end, the international opinion won out and Iguchi's actions remained a secret. He was ordered to destroy all of the computer disks that had copies of his previous letters. Iguchi said of the outcome, "They wanted to solve the problem without anyone getting hurt, meaning no one would be held responsible."

Iguchi penned his fifth and final confessional letter on August 7. It was written under direct instructions from Tsuda, a fact that would have dire consequences for Tsuda when the facts came to light. Iguchi was instructed to write a shorter version of his original confession, one that the bank could give to the Ministry of Finance. In the letter, Iguchi was to take full and sole responsibility for the losses; there was to be absolutely no mention of the bank in any sort of cover-up. In the event that the issue ever became public, the bank would use this letter to show that Iguchi acted alone, thus deflecting any blame away from the bank's management. Given that the other versions of his confession had been destroyed, there would be no evidence to implicate them in the future.

The next day, on August 8, Mr. Fujita, the CEO of Daiwa, performed the unpleasant task of informing the Japanese Ministry of Finance about the incident, despite earlier assurances to Iguchi that the information wouldn't reach that regulatory body until

November. Members of the firm's management team approached Iguchi and asked if he'd be willing to accept a job transfer to a Daiwa affiliate in Japan, an offer he readily accepted. He spent the remainder of the month buying back the missing securities and replacing them in the appropriate accounts. At this point, it seemed like he was going to get away with it.

The wheels came off the plan in September. On September 18, 1995, an anonymous source at Daiwa notified the Fed of illegal activity in the New York office, and sent a copy of Iguchi's confession letter to the Federal Bureau of Investigation on September 21. Two days later, several FBI vehicles arrived at Iguchi's home and took him into custody. He was placed under arrest.

Iguchi was interrogated about the letter he'd sent to the CEO and, after he signed a cooperation agreement with the U.S. authorities, he told them his tale. Following the questioning, a team of FBI agents descended on Daiwa's New York office and confiscated nearly 100 boxes of documents. It was the beginning of the end for Iguchi and Daiwa Bank. "I could have shredded all the documents, taken a two-week vacation instead and been in some obscure country where no one would ever find me," Iguchi later said, no doubt with a bitter mind. "I left myself wide-open legally. I had put Daiwa's interest ahead of my own." That was, after all, the Japanese way.

Daiwa attempted to appease federal authorities by taking proactive action against itself. The top 30 executives at the bank were forced to take a 30% reduction in pay for a period of six months, and they would forego their bonuses for the year. It was a self-imposed slap on the wrist at best. Fujita, the CEO, was forced to resign, as were his Deputy CEO Mr. Yasui and Senior Managing Director Mr. Yamaji. A new CEO was appointed from among the staff of the domestic division – that group realized its original goal in the end – and he immediately apologized for the poor management of the past, with a direct jab at the international division.

The American authorities were unimpressed with Daiwa's response and began their own examination of the fraud. Throughout the course of the FBI's investigation, auditors uncovered other instances of rogue trading and the effort to hide the losses. More important to their investigation, however, they discovered that Daiwa had reported the loss to the Japanese Ministry of Finance on August 8, whereas the Ministry claimed that they hadn't known anything until some time in September.

Robert Rubin, then Secretary of the Treasury, was apoplectic. Daiwa was one target of his rage, as the bank had waited to notify U.S. authorities of the fraud. Masayoshi Takemura, the Japanese Foreign Minister, was the other subject of his anger, and Rubin called Takemura to berate him for failing to inform the appropriate U.S. offices. It was a tremendous loss of face for Takemura, as he had no defense to offer. Instead, he was forced to sit and take the verbal barrage from his American counterpart.

Japanese officials in the Ministry of Finance were so worried about the humiliation that they sent two senior officials to Washington, D.C. to plead for leniency. Their efforts were in vain. On November 2, 1995, the Federal Reserve – together with six different states, the New York Banking Department (NYBD), and the Federal Deposit Insurance Corporation (FDIC) – issued a cease-and-desist order to Daiwa Bank, effective immediately. They were given until February 2, 1996 to comply, which meant closing their New York offices and winding down their U.S. operations.

But that was the tip of the metaphorical iceberg for Daiwa. Soon after, a federal grand jury in New York City handed down a 24-count criminal indictment against the bank, charging them with conspiracy and fraud in connection to the cover-up. The bank was facing up to $1.3 billion in fines. Takashi Kaiho, the newly-appointed CEO, called the indictments "very inappropriate," but his protestations fell on deaf ears. Daiwa Bank was fined $340 million – a record amount at the time – for its delay in reporting the unauthorized trading and subsequent attempts to cover it up. It was noted that a full two months passed before bank management notified U.S. authorities about the fraud. The judge in the case said in his opinion, "Daiwa Bank has acted with exceptional contempt of U.S. law and U.S. regulatory authority." As a result of the fine and the losses, Daiwa Bank was forced to sell $336 million in real estate holdings they had in Osaka, Tokyo, and Hiroshima.

Masahiro Tsuda, the General Manager of Daiwa's New York office, was charged with taking part in the conspiracy, a charge to which he pleaded guilty. As part of his arrangement with prosecutors, he received a two-month prison sentence and was forced to pay a fine of $100,000.

The trader who had started the whole downfall didn't get off quite so easily. His former employers turned on him with a vengeance. "We trusted him with everything, but he betrayed us," claimed former CEO Fujita. Deputy CEO Yasui echoed those sentiments: "We had great expectations of him, and so he felt obliged to keep going instead of coming clean." Another bank official took the opportunity to cast Iguchi as being something akin to fake Japanese: "He was a locally-hired employee. Our proper employees would never do such a thing."

Toshihide Iguchi pleaded guilty to conspiring with Daiwa's senior management in an attempt to conceal his losses, crimes that carried a potential for nine years in prison and a $3 million fine. At Iguchi's sentencing, his lawyer pleaded with the judge for a reduced sentence. "What motivated him, frankly, was a desire to save face," the attorney argued. Given that the judge was not himself Japanese, it is unlikely that he fully appreciated the gravity of losing face for Iguchi. He handed down a sentence of four years in prison, a $2.57 million fine, and Iguchi was required to forfeit all of his personal assets.

All things considered, it could be argued that Iguchi got off pretty lightly. When the final numbers were tallied, the number was beyond staggering. Starting with an initial loss of $70,000, Iguchi had managed to rack up a total deficit of $1.1 billion.

Following the Iguchi unpleasantness, the Daiwa Bank, Ltd. merged with the Asahi Bank, Ltd. in March of 2003. The new entity is now called the Resona Bank, Ltd. The name was derived from the Latin word *resonus*, meaning "resonate." The name was chosen because it was indicative of the new firm's desire to build strong ties with their customers by resonating with them. Ironically, one of the other definitions of the word resonate is "to receive a sympathetic response."

*   *   *

Iguchi served his four years at Allenwood Federal Correctional Institution in White Deer, Pennsylvania. During his time in prison, Iguchi was understandably depressed. In fact, his mood was so low at one point that a fellow inmate had to talk the former trader out of suicide, the only solution Iguchi saw for the profound loss of face. He also wrote a book in prison during his time in solitary confinement. He wrote it in his native Japanese, and it was published in January of 1997 and called simply *The Confession*. In it, Iguchi said that his motivation for writing it was that "I needed to redeem myself for my family and friends." It was an immediate best-seller in Japan.

He was released from prison in March of 1999. "I finally felt I had done all I could do to redeem myself as an honorable person," Iguchi said. He moved back to his hometown of Kobe in 2007, where he currently lives. He started his own company dedicated to the development of educational computer software, and has since written a second book, an update of *The Confession*, which is called *My Billion Dollar Education.*

Since returning to Japan, Iguchi has been on something of a one-man crusade to vilify bank culture, pointing to it as the root cause of his actions. "The government expected corporations to take care of themselves rather than report each little irregularity," he said. "In the U.S., the individual's loyalty belongs only to the individual, and the corporation's loyalty belongs only to the corporation. In Japan, the individual remains loyal to his company, and the individual companies maintain their loyalty to the government." In other words, it was a cultural division that caused his downfall.

To this day, Iguchi does not see himself as a criminal. In fact, he claims a sense of moral superiority over other rogue traders, like Nick Leeson, who was caught the same year as Iguchi. His claim to a higher level of morality stems from the fact that he confessed his crimes and didn't flee the country, unlike Leeson.

"The natural instinct for any trader is to hide the loss," Iguchi has said, in stark contrast to the hundreds of thousands of professional traders around the world who understand that losses are a part of the business. According to Iguchi, he's only guilty of violating internal bank rules and nothing more. Of course, he ignores the fact that he stole customer property. He still claims that it wasn't a crime because rogue traders "lack criminal intent." Rather, he argues that rogue traders "aren't doing this to enrich themselves. They are trying to get their jobs back."

Once again, it's all about saving face. It's that elusive thing that Lin Yutang said defied any attempts to fully translate. Without being immersed in the Japanese culture, no one can fully comprehend what it means. But, while there are certain nuances associated with Japanese culture, labeling face with the "lost in translation" tag is inaccurate.

What drove Iguchi was the same thing that drives other rogue traders to do what they do. It's ego, plain and simple. Losing face would have meant losing his reputation and that would have resulted in personal and public embarrassment. He is quick to point out that we shouldn't fault him, because hiding losses is "natural instinct" for a trader, but then he retreats to the safe haven of cultural differences to explain why he continued his fraud for so long.

Fraudulent deception is not a natural instinct for professional and reputable traders; ego, however, is a trait that everyone shares in common. None of us – traders or any other profession, for that matter – wants to be publicly embarrassed. At its core, Iguchi's years of illegal activity were the product of his ego.

Iguchi continues to cling to his defense, denying that he deserved punishment: "After all, losing a lot of money is not a crime, even if it was unauthorized." It's true, losing money is itself not a crime. However, he neglects the fact that he stole hundreds of millions of dollars' worth of property that belonged to someone else, and used the proceeds to help offset his losses. The second he took that first security from a customer account, it went from losing money to outright thievery. And that is illegal, even in Japan. But with his unyielding refusal to believe that he did anything wrong, Iguchi will never have the opportunity to learn from his past.

We can only hope that financial institutions don't share his tunnel vision, as there is an inestimable value to be gained from examining past mistakes. As we've been told before, those who don't learn from the past are condemned to repeat it. Financial institutions are served best to learn from mistakes of the past in order to keep an eye on the future. If the financial world allows personal pride – call it face, call it ego, call it whatever you like – to blind itself from seeing what is right and wrong, rogue traders will continue to operate.

YASUO HAMANAKA AND SUMITOMO, 1996

The man who would come to be known as "Mr. Copper," was born Yasuo Hamanaka in 1950. He attended Seikei University, a middle-of-the-road institution, where he studied, ironically enough, law. After graduation, he was hired by Sumitomo Corporation in April of 1970 to work in their non-ferrous metals division.

It was, by all accounts, a relatively non-descript job for a relatively non-descript man. He was a typical "salaryman" dressed in grey suits on the commuter train bound for Tokyo; he didn't stand out from the other men packed in alongside him in any way. He was a married father of two children who lived in the Tokyo suburbs and, at least by outward appearances, there was nothing extraordinary about him.

In April of 1973, he was assigned to Sumitomo's copper metals section and two years later was sent to the London to learn the finer points of trading copper at the LME, where he was buying and selling copper for the accounts of Sumitomo. By 1983, he was back at the Tokyo office and had been promoted to the position of full copper trader, trading upwards of 9,000 metric tons of copper a month, or just over 100,000 tons annually. Nothing out of the ordinary.

As Sumitomo's then head copper trader was scheduled to move on to a new assignment, Hamanaka was chosen to replace him, which put him solely in charge of the company's entire copper business. He would not only be buying and selling physical copper and copper futures contracts, but would also oversee the settlement of the trades - moving copper around the world and setting the prices between Sumitomo's suppliers and its customers. It was, to be sure, a fantastic opportunity for a man who hadn't distinguished himself in anyway, except perhaps as a testament to his incredible work ethic.

Hamanaka walked into his new assignment assuming he was inheriting a vastly profitable part of the Sumitomo's trading arm, but his assumption quickly proved wrong. Soon after arriving, he learned that the copper desk was carrying a $50 million loss, and, the man who most people couldn't pick out of a crowd of weary salarymen, would end up doing everything he possibly could over the next ten years to cover up the loss he'd inherited.

*　　*　　*

Historians believe that copper was first extracted from the earth around 9,000 B.C. The official name came much later though, derived from the Latin word *cyprium*, or "metal of Cyprus," which was then shortened to *cuprum* by the Romans. And it's from there that we get the modern-day word. The Romans, along with many others, valued copper for both its beauty and functionality. The metal in its pure form is malleable - it can be stretched, molded, and shaped, which made it easily used for early coinage. Then, there's that unique property that's even more appealing - it's a biostatic metal, meaning bacteria will not grow on it. For those reasons, copper is a highly-valued metal for industrial uses, which also makes it a very attractive investment opportunity.

Copper, however, also has a flawed characteristic of tarnishing when it's exposed to sulfides, giving its surface a green tarnish. That's the look we see on the Statue of Liberty, leading to the often-used term "tarnished copper," and it's become the accepted look of copper that's old and weathered. Interestingly, that tarnished color posed something of a problem when the statue was repaired in the mid-1980s. The new copper hadn't yet been exposed to the elements, so curators were forced to paint the new surface to match the weathered color of the old Lady Liberty.

In modern times, copper became even more important because it has very high thermal and electrical conductivity, making it the ideal metal for electrical products. The metal is, in fact, the second-highest in conductivity among pure metals, ranking only behind silver, and therefore more economical for industrial purposes due to the relatively high cost of silver.

There are major copper reserves in the United States, though the Andean region in South America is the largest known depository. These days, South America accounts for about 45% of the world's copper production, with Chile providing about 33% of the overall supply. The major copper mining companies include Rio Tinto Group, Anglo American PLC and Glencore International AG, all well-known names around the world. Ayn Rand even used copper in her epic book *Atlas Shrugged* in the character of Francisco d'Anconia, the playboy heir to his father's copper mine fortune.

Getting copper from the ground to the end-user isn't easy - it's a long and complicated process. After being extracted from a mine, the copper ore goes to a smelter. There it's processed, with all of the extraneous materials being removed from the ore, leaving behind the pure copper. It's then sold and shipped directly from the producers to the consumers, mostly industrial companies located in the United

States, Europe and Asia. It's similar to the distribution of most other commodities, except the volume and weight of the copper shipments makes the process incredibly expensive and time-consuming.

The demand for copper fluctuates like any commodity, with price spikes generally coming during times of war and global industrial booms. During the Vietnam War, for instance, copper demand temporarily peaked at a price of 57 cents per pound. That price continued to climb over the years, going to 77 cents per pound in 1974 and up to 84 cents in 1981. By the end of the 1980s, the price of copper started its modern rise, doubling to $1.68 in 1988 and continuing on from there.

The fluctuating price has a huge impact on the cost of everyday consumer goods. Copper is a major component in plumbing fixtures such as pipes, manufactured goods such as refrigerators, as well as wiring in high-tech electronic goods. The average automobile contains nearly a mile of copper wiring, and the typical small car uses 44 pounds of the metal. For a typical hybrid vehicle, that amount balloons to 99 pounds.

And while all financial instruments experience price changes from day to day, the copper market is one that is especially characterized by price fluctuations – often quite volatile fluctuations, at that. The volatility in prices drives both producers and consumers to hedge themselves against those price fluctuations. And hedging is where the futures market comes into play. The price swings in copper mean that a savvy investor who knows what he's doing stands to make a financial killing, if he plays the market right. And as we have seen – and as we shall see countless times again – any time there is an opportunity to make a great deal of money, there will inevitably be someone in the market who pushes his luck just a little too far.

*   *   *

Though copper is a commodity that's physically bought and sold all around the world, its price is essentially set in just one place - the London Metal Exchange (LME). The LME was established in 1876 when Great Britain was the hub of the world's international commerce and finance. It began as a market solely to bring together the metal consumers in Europe with the producers in Peru and Chile. The exchange provided the metals mining and trading firms with a way to hedge the price of their shipments from South America to Europe through forward contracts.

Today, the LME remains the pivotal center for pricing metals, with 95% of the LME trading volume in non-ferrous metals, including: aluminum, zinc, nickel, tin and copper. But, of all the metals traded, the LME's most important market is copper. During copper trading's hey-days in the 1990s, it was *the* most traded metal on the LME, with 88% of all copper contracts in the world trading on the exchange, leaving the remaining volume to the rival exchange in New York City, the COMEX, or Commodities Exchange.

Back in the 1990s, there was major difference between the two exchanges. The LME was a traditional and loosely regulated market, whereas the COMEX was a more tightly regulated startup. There was no mandatory position reporting on the LME, nor were any statistics published about the open interest, like exactly who owns how much. Most metals trading firms could do what they wanted on the LME, without, let's say, the prying eyes of pesky officials looking over their shoulders. Another important difference between the two is that the COMEX is a futures exchange, with all of the trades between the members facing the exchange; whereas at the LME, the members faced each other directly.

The traditions at the LME harkened back to the old days of the open-outcry exchanges. Four times a day during the trading day, copper is traded for five minute periods – located in "the ring" – where well-dressed traders in three-piece pin-stripped suits scream back-and-forth at one another for a full 300 seconds. When the trading period ends, the traders walk quietly out of the ring and another group prepares for their metal's furious price setting. That chaotic scene is what determines the price of copper worldwide. The final bid and offer price at the end of the second ring becomes the official price on the exchange – the price used to determine approximately 90% of the world's copper.

When copper futures and forward prices are quoted, the specific grade of copper referenced is called Grade A Electrolytic Copper Cathodes. It's a scientific way of saying incredibly large sheets of highly-conductive copper, and they're quoted in cents-per-ton for huge amounts – measured in metric tons – of the metal.

Most of the contracts traded on the LME are called "three-month forwards," the contracts that call for the delivery of physical copper in three months. These were always the most actively traded contracts because, historically, it took about three months for copper to be shipped from South America, where it was produced, to an LME warehouse in Europe. When the contract is due, the seller is required to deliver the specified amount into an exchange-approved warehouse to the buyer.

The importance of warehouses can't be understated. The LME does not own the warehouses themselves; the exchange only serves as the final authority in approving the storage facilities used for contract deliveries. A seller of a copper forward contract, when it expires, has to either have it on hand at the warehouse, buy it from someone who owns it at the warehouse, borrow it from someone who owns it, or have it delivered in from an outside source.

Regardless of where the copper comes from, in order to fulfill the exchange's contractual obligations, a copper seller must ensure that the designated amount of copper is at the designated warehouse at the designated time. Period. Failure to do so risks losing the member's seat on the exchange, not to mention severe financial penalties. That means that anyone who could control the supply of copper in the LME warehouses could effectively dictate the price of the metal, and that means dictating price of copper throughout the world.

What's even more important about the warehouses is that, despite the fact that they're scattered throughout the globe, there's a very finite amount of copper in them at any particular time. In other words, between five- and ten-percent of the world's copper supply is housed at the warehouses on any given day. While the global size of the copper market is valued at nearly $1.5 trillion, someone only needs to own the amount stored in the warehouses to dictate the world's copper price. Theoretically, a single copper trader could corner the world's copper market by just controlling the amount in the warehouses. And that's exactly what would happen.

*   *   *

Sumitomo Shoji Kaisha, Ltd. was founded in the 16th century, shortly after Sumitomo Masatomo learned silver and copper smelting techniques from Western traders. Sumitomo opened his first mine – the Besshi Copper Mine – in 1691, which firmly established his firm in the years to come as one of Japan's oldest and proudest companies. The founding principles that guided the newly-created firm's operations were written down by the founder himself and codified in a philosophy he called Monjuin Shiigaki. It consisted of two articles. Article 1 dictated, "Sumitomo shall achieve strength and prosperity by placing prime importance on integrity and sound management in the conduct of its business." Article 2 was equally brief and to the point, declaring, "Sumitomo shall manage its activities with foresight and flexibility in order to cope effectively with the changing times. Under no circumstances, however, shall it pursue easy gains or act imprudently."

Sumitomo would later expand its business into a host of other areas, including medicine, forestry, machinery, coal, chemicals, construction and electrical cable. But copper was still the source of the firm's income and growth. It was the foundiation on which the company was built. And, as industry developed and the use of copper increased, Japan became one of the world's largest copper consumers.

The name of the firm was officially changed to Sumitomo Corporation in 1978, and quickly established itself as the largest copper trading firm in the world, supplying mostly copper cathode to Asian customers. By the mid-1990s, Sumitomo Corporation boasted annual sales of $133 billion with $34.8 billion in assets, and had 154 offices on five continents.

As the firm proudly attributed its dominance in the world of global copper trading to "expertise in risk management," and part of that risk management involved hedging the ups and downs of the price of copper. After all, they were involved in every step of the process, from purchasing physical copper to transporting and selling it. That made them vulnerable to price fluctuations, a vulnerability they hedged by trading copper futures and forward contracts.

*   *   *

In November of 1985, Hamanaka was officially promoted to the position of Assistant General Manager of the Nonferrous Metals

Division. He was the de-facto head trader of the copper desk, but he was still waiting for the current head trader, Saburo "Steve" Shimizu to move on to his new position. Upon arriving at his desk, with the utmost optimism, he was confronted with, what can only be called, a great disappointment. He was informed by Shimizu that they were carrying a loss on their books. A very large loss, in fact. And there was one more catch, it hadn't yet been disclosed to those higher up on the org chart. It was the last thing Hamanaka expected.

The loss came from a copper trade done by Shimizu in which he bought physical copper in the Philippines, just when the price took a nosedive. Shimizu had been spending all of his time trying to trade out of the loss, which had reached $50 million by March 1986.

Both men agreed that the loss was "too great" to tell their superiors and they decided to keep the shortfall a secret. Shimizu would later testify in court that he had advised Hamanaka that the only way to recoup the loss would be through "unauthorized futures trading."

In August of 1987, Hamanaka's title was officially changed, cementing him as the head of the copper team, with the still-undisclosed loss that had grown to $58 million. Shimizu was reassigned to the Sumitomo office in Manila and shortly thereafter resigned from the company, accepting a position as a copper broker with Rudolf Wolff & Company, leaving Hamanaka on his own.

With the same hubris that afflicts so many rogue traders, Hamanaka was convinced that he could make back the loss, given enough time to do so. It was just a matter of trading the market. After all, his position at Sumitomo afforded him a great deal of knowledge about the movements in the price of copper. The firm's dominant position clearly gave him the competitive edge he needed to make back the money.

Sumitomo had a tremendous amount of copper on hand at any given time because of the agreements to sell physical copper to their customers. By finding a way to push copper prices higher, he figured he could earn the money back and wipe out the loss. Just by moving the price of copper a little higher, it meant his customers would pay a higher price, and, in a way, his customers would cover the loss. All Hamanaka had to do was drive up the price in the LME ring and that wouldn't be too difficult given that all he had to do was control 5% to 10% of the copper kept in the warehouses. The plan was simple and a good trading idea, at least on paper.

The next year, in 1988, Hamanaka began acquiring copper on the LME, but immediately, news started to trickle out via various reporting agencies. There was nothing suspicious about what he was doing; it was simply a copper trader doing what he got paid to do. The main problem was that well-known Sumitomo already owned huge amounts of the metal. When the largest copper player in the world is buying, it's news. It also confirmed what Hamanaka already knew - news of Sumitomo buying more copper just sent prices higher, leaving him owning more copper at an inflated price. He realized he was just too visible a player to move the price discretely on his own. He needed someone to work with.

From 1989 until 1992, Hamanaka began actively discussed how he could manipulate the copper market, at first with a well-known metals trader named R. David Campbell. Campbell was somewhat of the go-to guy in the metals markets. He had started his career at Amalgamated Metals Corp back in the early 1970s, where he learned the ins and outs of the metals business. When he left Amalgamated, he took $400 and opened his own trading account. Fast-forward ten years and Campbell had proven himself as one of the best metals traders in the industry. According to industry veterans, he was one of those guys who just knew how always make money and often described as "a very clever guy." By the late 1980s he was living the Wall Street dream. A successful trader with a seven room apartment in New York City's Sutton Place and would later build a 10,000+ square foot house in the Hamptons on Georgica pond; an estate of 25 acres.

The pair agreed that Hamanaka needed to get a group of others involved. It had to be a very special group: traders and brokers who were confortable operating in the grey areas of the market. By working together, they would, in turn, help Hamanaka create the appearance of an artificial shortage and drive the price higher. The others involved would buy and sell for him, so it wouldn't look like Hamanaka was doing the buying. When they finally owned a sufficient amount in the LME warehouses, it would appear there was a shortage, and prices would move higher.

His counterparties also needed to be willing to alter the details of the trades so Hamanaka could hide the actual size of his own position. Officially, he wasn't allowed to speculatively drive up copper prices at Sumitomo. Falsifying trade confirmations would make it appear that his purchases were aimed at "hedging" existing sales, but at the same time, he'd be building up more and more control over the copper market.

It was, to be sure, a highly complex and illegal scheme. Hamanaka sought out willing and able counterparties and right away found one: Rudolf Wolff & Company.

Rudolf Wolff was, ironically enough, Saburo Shimizu's employer, the man responsible for the original loss. Shimizu had no problem providing Hamanaka with the numerous false documents he needed, including trade confirmations that never happened and invoices that had been altered. Rudolf Wolff was open for business, as long as the price was right.

With the large amount of copper that Hamanaka needed to hide, he still needed other players to assist him, so he enlisted the Zambia Consolidated Copper Mines, Limited (ZCCM). Beginning in the 1970s, the Republic of Zambia began a nationalization campaign to drive out foreign domination of their vast collection of copper mines. By 1982, all of the copper mines were consolidate into one majority-owned government company named ZCCM. Part of the remaining ownership was in the hands of Rhodesian Selection Trust, or RST, and long-time copper trading firm with offices around the global. The President of the New York RST office was none other than David Campbell.

Year after year, the Zambians never produced enough copper to fulfill their sales contracts and often needed to buy copper themselves. Because of that, ZCCM[1] was also more than happy to assist; showing copper to have been bought, shipped and sold, despite the fact that it never moved anywhere. Basically, it started with ZCCM booking the sale of physical copper to RST[2]. The RST, in turn, sold the copper to Sumitomo, who then either sold it to Chinese customers or sold it right back to ZCCM to help fulfill their over-sales. On the books, everything appeared legitimate, the copper paper trail essentially began with a mining company and finished with a end-user. In reality, the timing of the transactions allowed Hamanaka to control that copper for a period of time.

These transactions provided Hamanaka with the justification he needed to hedge the copper he was holding at the LME. He was showing sales of copper going out to RST and the mining company in Zambia, just in case anyone within Sumitomo or at the exchanges started poking around.

The first sign of trouble came when Hamanaka approached a metals brokerage firm named DLT, Inc., based in Randolph, Vermont. David Threlkeld, the owner of the firm, got his start in the business, ironically enough, at Rudolf Wolff & Company. Threlkeld started DLT in 1983 out of his country home in Vermont and, by 1991, he had offices in London and Tokyo, employing Ashley Levett, Charles Vincent, Paul Shuter, Terry Willsone,

---

[1] ZCCM booked these transactions through its subsidiary, MEMACL, which basically stood for Metal Marketing Company

[2] Though ZCCM was willing to help out Hamanaka, based on Japanese business practice, Zambia was not within Sumitomo's sphere of influence. In Japan, the country of Zambia belonged to Mitsubishi, so Hamanaka could not deal with ZCCM directly without breaking Japanese business ethics

Peter Montrose, and Paul Scully. Rumors – the bane of a trader's existence, especially one who is about to go rogue – had begun to circulate about Sumitomo in the copper market for months. Though they were only amorphous whisperings, they suddenly became concrete when Hamanaka called Threlkeld on the phone and asked if DLT would be willing to work with him. Specifically, Hamanaka wanted DLT to back-date trade confirmations worth about $425 million, trades which never had taken place. Threlkeld said he was unaware of the trades but would look into the matter, Hamanaka responded, "Don't bother because they don't exist."

Soon after, Threlkeld received a hand-written letter from Hamanaka asking him again to submit false trade confirms. The letter was written on Sumitomo corporate stationary and signed with Hamanaka's trademark "Y. Hamanaka" signature. In the letter, Hamanaka explained that it was nothing more than "a special request for our company's internal accounting purposes only." It went on to say, "I guarantee that this will not cause you any trouble." In closing, it was requested that the confirmations be sent to a "Mr. Nishi" in Tokyo.

Threlkeld flat-out refused to help in the scheme, saying he wouldn't "confirm details of nonexistent trades." He took it a step further and reported Hamanaka's ethical breach to the LME. The authorities at the LME were understandably quite concerned and contacted Sumitomo directly for "clarification" on the matter. The responder from Sumitomo, who was clearly oblivious to what Hamanaka was doing, denied any wrongdoing. David King, the CEO of the LME, still took it one step further and summoned Hamanaka and his boss to the LME offices in London. After exchanging pleasantries and business cards, Hamanaka explained that Sumitomo was engaging in a series of transactions to avoid Japanese taxes. To King, it was a matter outside of their jurisdiction, so no further action was taken. And the matter was closed. Years later, when the U.K.'s

Serious Fraud Office was investigating the matter, they asked King how he knew the man with Hamanaka was his boss. King explained that the man had the right business card, though strangely, didn't speak a word of English and Hamanaka did all of the translating.

Though Threlkeld wasn't willing to work with Hamanaka, it didn't mean some of his employees were going to ignore a good opportunity when they saw it. Soon afterwards, Ashley Levett and Charles Vincent set up Winchester Commodities, in the town of Winchester just southeast of London, taking with them Paul Shuter. It was there at Winchester where Charlie Vincent would earn the nickname "Copper Fingers" by many in the industry. In British slang, someone going by the moniker "fingers" is never a compliment, since it implies some kind of shady dealing. The three of them together set out to poach Threlkeld's business and they had no problem doing everything that Threlkeld wouldn't. Their first call upon setting up shop went straight to Hamanaka. They would become front-men for Hamanaka, buying and selling his copper contracts and getting paid a share of the profits from whatever copper price appreciation they helped arrange. Over the course of the next few years, Winchester would reap a reported $50 million[3] for their assistance.

It didn't end there for Threlkeld, however. For his efforts at attempting to preserve the integrity of the LME, he was blacklisted from doing business at the LME for making what was termed a "false accusation." Though not official, many LME members just flat-out refused to do business with him. Clearly, no one at the LME wanted to annoy the exchange's largest customer, Hamanaka. Soon after, Threlkeld's last loyal employee, Paul Scully, died in what was quickly ruled an accidental fire.

Smarting from the blow he'd taken at the LME, the death of Scully, and the loss of all of his employees, Threlkeld took his problems

---

[3] One inside source told me the $50 million figure "is a dramatic understatement."

directly to the Securities and Futures Authority (SFA), the British regulatory agency with authority over the LME. In addition to the letter, Threlkeld included a report of a copper futures trade of 20,000 metric tons valued at $80 million that Hamanaka had transacted at off-market prices. Again, quickly enough, the matter was dropped.

By now, however, Hamanaka already had enough ready-and-willing conspirators to play along with his scheme. He could easily hide the size of his copper positions and had control of Sumitomo's LME futures contracts and their physical copper inventories, but it wasn't enough to sufficiently move the price of the metal itself. He still needed a way to buy more physical copper, which meant that he needed to borrow money to finance those purchases. Almost all of the pieces were in place to corner the copper market. If successful, he'd make a killing.

*   *   *

As the calendar page flipped to January of 1993, the price of copper was sitting at $1.0742 per pound. Hamanaka was working on ways to borrow the cash he needed to buy more copper. The problem was that he couldn't just borrow money in Sumitomo's name, as it would alert corporate executives that he was doing something out of the ordinary. He didn't have the authority to issue corporate debt or arrange a loan from a third party, so he needed to find another way.

The solution was relatively simple, actually, and it was pretty brilliant. He realized he could sell copper put options that were out-of-the-money. In other words, selling someone the right to sell him copper at prices below the current market price. He'd collect the options premiums from the buyers and use that money to purchase more copper. That's the simple part of it, and it's a common technique used by rogue traders when scrambling to come up with quick cash.

The brilliant component comes when you consider what he was trying to do in the first place - drive up the price of copper. There was no doubt in his mind that he'd move copper prices higher and those put options would expire worthless. Knowing that, the put options buyers, suckers as they were, would clearly lose all of their money. Ironically, he was using money from the people betting against him to guarantee they'd lose their bets. It was as close to a risk-free way of earning money as he could ever think of; it was a financial manipulation scheme at its best.

With a boatload of put options sold, Hamanaka set to work trading enormous amounts of copper, moving around trades of 500,000 tons at any one time. The huge number of contracts is what earned him the nickname of "Mr. Copper," and his positions amounted to about five percent of the world's copper supply. Remember, too, this was a man who, when he started trading copper, barely eclipsed 100,000 tons a year. Now he was doing five times that amount in a single trade. As he expected, he was able to move the price of copper higher and it looked like his genius plan was working. By the middle of the year, there appeared to be an actual shortage of copper, all because of the control of the copper ring that Hamanaka held. All the while, copper supplies were tucked neatly away in Sumitomo's warehouse accounts.

Then, *The Financial Times* reported on August 3, 1993 about "the 'squeeze' threatening to create turmoil on the LME market in September and October 1993." A trader was quoted in the article saying that "Sumitomo had reached a position where if it were October today, it would control all the LME [copper] stocks." Suddenly, Hamanaka was looking like a genius. He was going to make a fortune, and he was already planning to replicate his scheme again the next year.

But there's a potential problem inherent in trying to squeeze any market, and that's regulatory interference. British market rules dictated that regulatory agencies and authorities can intervene if there's a shortage that threatens to drive prices up too high or too quickly. Things like suspending contract delivery specifications, allowing delivery of a lower quality product, and allowing additional warehouses to make good deliveries. And that is exactly what happened in September 1993.

The LME intervened due to the spike in copper prices and the price dropped considerably. By the end of the year, the price of copper was down to $0.9156, lower than it began at the beginning of the year, despite Hamanaka's efforts to drive it higher. Suddenly those out-of-the-money put options were in-the-money, which meant that Hamanaka was now on the hook for buying the copper from those "suckers" who bought the options in the first place. As a result, he took a $393 million loss.

Hamanaka arranged a loan from ING Bank for $100 million by forging the signature of his senior manager. He'd worry about paying the money back when the time came. Credit Lyonnais Rouse, the LME member that cleared Sumitomo's trades on the exchange, apologized for their role in driving up prices and agreed to pay the LME £100,000 for the costs the exchange incurred. Officially it wasn't a fine, but it sure looked that way to everyone else.

And even though his first attempt at squeezing the market ended in a colossal failure, Hamanaka was not put off. In fact, though his losses had just grown substantially, he rationalized that the problem had been simply a matter of size. In short, he hadn't owned enough copper to push the price high enough. If he were able to accumulate more physical copper the next year, he reasoned, then all of the pieces would be in place for his plan to work perfectly.

In 1994, Hamanaka joined forces again with David Campbell, the man who originally gave him the roadmap for his manipulation plan, but this time the partnership went beyond strategic discussions. Campbell had moved from RST to become the President of a thinly-capitalized start-up firm named Global Minerals And Metals Corporation (GMMC), which had recently been formed in January 1994 with four partners. The express purpose of GMMC was for one thing: to assist Hamanaka in the copper market.

On paper, GMMC looked like a full-service metals trading company. It was run by Campbell, had a chief trader named Carl Alm, and was made up of a group of other former RST employees. Initially, it was rumored that Campbell had developed a computer algorithm to trade the copper market. However, with or without a computer, everyone in the copper market knew he was very good at trading the metals markets. Campbell even arranged for a former Zambian government official to work for them as a consultant. This consultant would, not surprisingly, line up a lucrative contract for GMMC to buy copper from ZCCM.

Sumitomo was not a member of the LME, and therefore had no direct relationship with the exchange. Instead, they did their trading through LME members. Metals brokering and trading firms, like GMMC, Rudolf Wolf, and Winchester Commodities, arranged trades for Hamanaka and then the trades cleared through a member of the exchange. None of these firms had an actual seat on the exchange and they executed their trades through REFCO Securities and other LME members.

The relationship between all of the firms was strictly confidential. Nobody outside of the actual participants knew that Hamanaka, Rudolf Wolf, Winchester, and GMMC were working together. In fact, the Hamanaka relationship was so well managed inside GMMC that only Campbell and Alm knew the extent of what was going on. Under the guise of legitimacy, GMMC would buy and sell copper on the exchanges, all the while acting as a front for Hamanaka. GMMC had arranged a very lucrative deal for themselves with Hamanaka.

Campbell wasn't a philanthropist doing this out of his own innate generosity. He expected to be paid for his efforts, and there was a contract[4] in place to guarantee him both money and security. At the beginning of every copper trading season, Campbell and Hamanaka would agree on a floor price for copper. That is, they would set a minimum price at which Hamanaka would buy copper throughout the year from GMMC, basically guaranteeing that Campbell wouldn't lose money. In exchange, if the price of copper exceeded the floor price, Hamanaka would buy copper from GMMC and each get a share of the appreciation. On paper, it was a great deal for Hamanaka. From GMMC's perspective, the lucrative part of the deal was the price floor. They could keep the profits they made trading copper and always knew they could sell to Hamanaka at the fixed floor price. For a trader, having a buyer at a certain price is extremely valuable.

On top of that, GMMC knew in advance when the largest copper trader in the world was buying and selling. It was, quite possibly, the best financial trade profit-sharing agreement ever created, at least for Campbell. All they had to worry about was the legal ramifications.

Now that GMMC had a copper buyer, the next step was to arrange a similar deal with a copper producer. Campbell then reached out to the large government-run Chilean copper producer named CODELCO.

CODELCO, in English, stands for the National Copper Corporation of Chile. It was formed in 1976 when Chile placed all of their nationalized copper mines into one government-run corporation. By the 1990s, it was the largest copper producer

---

[4] GMMC set a "floor price" with Hamanaka at the beginning of the season. As long as copper was below the floor price, GMMC sold copper to Hamanaka at the floor price (per ton). Once the price exceeded the "floor price," Hamanaka bought at the market price plus $35 less a 30% of the difference between the market price and the floor price. So, if the copper price was greater than the floor price, then Hamanaka bought at the market price + $35 - [(market price - floor price) * 30%]

in the world, supplying the global with about 11% of its copper needs. COLDELCO, like other government-run corporations, had plenty of former executives looking to make a little extra money after years of government service. Campbell did what everyone else did, he hired three of them.

Campbell arranged a similar deal[5] with CODELCO. As a copper producer, they naturally wanted the highest price for the copper they produced and wanted to hedge against prices going lower. Campbell, knowing he had a buyer, negotiated the deal with CODELCO. He would set a base price for CODELCO with a similar profit sharing agreement if the price of copper appreciated. Once again, it looked like CODELCO got the deal of the century too. Campbell, knowing Hamanaka was going to move prices higher, also stood to make a second financial killing from CODELCO if copper prices moved higher.

With GMMC to assist him, Hamanaka still needed some capital to accomplish his plan. For an average person, when that individual wants a loan, he generally goes to a bank. After some fact-checking and analysis of the person's credit, he gets the money he needs. It's essentially the same principle for a business. However, the metals division at Sumitomo couldn't just go out and borrow money to finance their commodity positions. Hamanaka, though, devised a plan to get what he needed.

He could borrow money by lending the metal itself through what are called metal swaps. It's a sale of the metal with an agreement to buy it back in the future, pretty similar to repo, or repurchase

---

[5] GMMC set a "base price" with CODELCO, about 10% higher than the floor price with Hamanaka. As long as copper was below the base price, GMMC bought CODELCO copper at the market price (per ton). Once the price exceeded the "base price," CODELCO received the "base price" plus $25 plus a 20% premium on the difference between the market price and the base price. So, if Copper > base price, then CODELCO received the "base price" + $25 + [(market price – base price) * 20%]

agreement, in the bond market. It's effectively a collateralized loan, with another party holding onto Sumitomo's copper as collateral against the loan. The great part about it was that the transactions were virtually impossible for Sumitomo's auditors to detect - they were recorded on the books as a sale with a re-purchase at a future date. Just like a repo transaction, there was a sale on one day and a purchase at a future date. It was pretty much what Hamanaka was supposed to do - buy and sell copper. Presumably at a profit.

The metal swaps were funneled through a single account that was opened at Merrill Lynch in the name of Sumitomo. It was designated the "Merrill Lynch B Account" and backed by the full faith and credit of Sumitomo Corporation. It was the largest trading line ever given by Merrill[6] to one of their customers and it was said to be in excess of $1 billion. Most importantly, GMMC had trading authority under it.

It's important to understand the role that Merrill Lynch played; they weren't just simple passive observers. Merrill knowingly advised and assisted Hamanaka with what he was doing. They had their own proprietary trading desk, dedicated to the buying and selling of copper, and that desk made a lot of money because they knew what Hamanaka was up to. Merrill clearly turned a blind eye by providing the rogue trader with the necessary money he needed to build his copper position, all for the sake of knowing just when he was buying and selling. Funny enough, Global Metals and Hamanaka knew that Merrill was front-running them, but turn a blind eye to it. As long as everyone was making money, no one wanted to rock the boat.

As Hamanaka was now able to acquire more copper, he drove the price up to $1.1105, an increase of nearly 20 cents since the beginning of the year. Through his partnership with GMMC he

---

[6] Up until that time

maintained a controlling position in LME warehouse stocks, with a large portion of that withheld from the market. The price of physical copper kept reaching higher and higher levels. And then the dominoes started to fall.

The first major financial disaster struck when the Chilean copper company CODELCO lost $206.8 million. A loss they initially flat-out attributed to a consortium in the copper market headed by Sumitomo. Philip Adeane, the managing director of Chile's Los Pelambres copper mine, placed the blame squarely on the shoulders of Yasuo Hamanaka, claiming that he "kept the price of copper at an unrealistic level for over a year." In reality, CODELCO's in-house copper trader, a man named Juan Pablo Davila, had been spec trading the copper market on his own. Davila was supposed to be hedging CODELCO's copper deliveries when, in fact, that hedging morphed into outright speculation. Davila claimed an initial hedging loss led him into more losses as he tried to make back the first loss, all the while the market continued to move higher against him. Davila would later be accused of accepting payments from his brokers and maintaining a secret account in the Cayman Islands. Ironically, Hamanaka's manipulation led to a rogue trader story within the rogue trader story.

Despite the fact that he successfully pushed the price of copper higher, Hamanaka was still facing his own financial demons. He was struggling to keep the price inflated, adding more and more copper to his already mammoth inventory. As money was pouring out, he was desperate to hide the outflow and he fell back on his old strategy of selling put options to raise some immediate capital. Surprisingly, the price of copper began to decline again, resulting in another $150 million loss for Hamanaka. But that didn't slow him down, as he still had an ace up his sleeve – the Merrill Lynch B Account and his metal swap agreements.

By the fall of 1994, Sumitomo owned 780,000 metric tons of copper in the Merrill Lynch B Account, as well as 1.3 million metric tons of forward copper contracts on the LME. The price was hovering around $1.13 in September, just when the annual mating season arrived. In the copper market, the mating season comes around in the autumn. It's the time when copper producers and buyers meet to negotiate the terms of their supply contracts for the coming year. It was the perfect time to push up prices, and guarantee higher prices for Sumitomo's Asian copper clients.

After they got through the mating season of 1994, Hamanaka sold 600,000 metric tons to booked some profits on his LME trades, but Hamanaka still owned way too much physical copper. Taking profits on the forward contracts had sent the price lower. The losses were mounting and Hamanaka's desperation grew with those losses. In November, he moved $770 million from Sumitomo's Hong Kong subsidiary under the pretense of paying for a trade, but in reality, that money was just to cover up losses.

Hamanaka just couldn't seem to do anything right. Every time he pushed up the price of copper, he lost money in the end. The original loss of $50 million in 1986 turned into a $393 million loss in 1993, which turned into a $770 million loss in 1994. The largest player in the world's copper market just couldn't seem to make any money trading copper. Somehow, he was consistently losing money from falling prices every time he tried driving prices higher.

*   *   *

The number three has both good and bad connotations. Whereas the third strike in baseball means you're out and bad things are said to come in threes, it's also been said that the third time's a charm. Hamanaka had failed miserably in his first two attempts at squeezing the copper market and his third, and final attempt, would come in 1995. Regardless of your feelings on the number three, Hamanaka would have been wise to remember that old saying about bad things coming in threes.

Early in 1995, Sumitomo Corporation floated the idea to the LME that they open a copper warehouse in the United States, something the LME had wanted to do for some time. It would, at least from the LME's perspective, allow them to better compete with the American-based COMEX exchange. From Hamanaka's perspective, it would give him the chance to grab some of the copper supplies in the U.S. market. The first American LME warehouse opened in Long Beach, California, and soon after, Hamanaka owned 39,000 metric tons of the copper stored there. By that spring, he'd also amassed a long position in forward copper contracts on the LME totaling approximately 2 million metric tons. All told, Sumitomo Corporation – or, more specifically, Hamanaka – now owned 50% of all copper supplies in all of the LME warehouses around the world. It was shaping up to be the copper play he always wanted.

Hamanaka and Campbell sat down to discuss a strategy for unwinding their position. The goal at the end of the day was, after all, to make money, not just to acquire more and more copper. The pair decided to set a target price. When copper reached that magic number, they would liquidate their positions, dumping as much as they could onto the inflated market. Now, keep in mind, anyone with advance knowledge of this plan could make a killing - riding the price appreciation all the way up and short-selling it on the way down. Knowledge of the plan was the equivalent of a trader's dream - knowing a market was going up, hitting a specific price and then declining. But the pair still had a long way to go before they got there.

By this time, Hamanaka was no longer the salaryman that he had been at the beginning of his career. He had a large ego and dressed in expensive western suits and ties, years before they became de rigueur in Tokyo business fashion. Hamanaka was enjoying the good life and was well-known at expensive Tokyo bars, like at the swanky Okura Hotel in Tokyo. To complete his image as a major player in the markets, he had begun going by a new nickname, this time "Mr. 5%," a name given to him by none other than his own boss at Sumitomo. The name was a direct reference to the fact that he owned 5% of the world's copper supply. When one metals industry veteran met him in Tokyo, Hamanaka flat out told him, "Of course, you have to remember I am not like the traders at the other Japanese house you know. I am the only one who understands our copper position."

In June 1995, Hamanaka wanted to open a credit line at J.P. Morgan, but once again, he couldn't let his superiors know about the account. That presented something of a problem, because the powers that be at J.P. Morgan in Tokyo wanted to meet him and his boss at their office. Hamanaka found the perfect solution. He grabbed a bunch of his boss' business cards, recruited his favorite bartender at the Okura Hotel in Tokyo, dressed him up in an expensive suit and brought him along for the meeting with J.P. Morgan. Of course, his new "boss" didn't speak any English, just nodded enthusiastically throughout the meeting. Hamanaka arranged the credit line from J.P. Morgan with the ability to finance up to $400 million worth of copper.

Hamanaka then reverted back to his metal swaps and borrowed money from the Merrill Lynch B Account, as well as obtaining a new $500 million credit line from Chase Manhattan Bank. He disguised the loans from the prying eyes of would-be internal auditors by calling them "a series of copper transactions," which he figured was vague enough to hide the metal swaps agreements, while still being specific enough to sound like they were legitimate.

That same month, it was estimated that Hamanaka controlled as much as 70% of all deliverable copper on both the LME and

COMEX exchanges, and, it was common knowledge among the metals industry that he was going to keep pushing the price higher. The global price of copper was now essentially controlled by one man, Yasuo Hamanaka. Copper hit an all-time of $1.475 and surpassed even the elusive price target that Hamanaka and Campbell had been aiming for. It was supposed to be the time to start liquidating, but then the three-headed monster of greed appeared. Both men figured that, since they already owned 70% of the supply, they might as well shoot for the moon and try to acquire it all. The original price target seemed like pocket change now.

Campbell advised Hamanaka to take delivery of some copper forward contracts that were scheduled to settle in late summer as a way of executing their domination plan. The team wanted to create the impression that Sumitomo had a huge need for copper in the fourth quarter of 1995, right at the beginning of the mating season. When the forward contracts came due on October 17, they began taking delivery into the Merrill Lynch B Account.

By November 24, Hamanaka controlled 93% of all LME warehouse stocks of copper, and that control continued through December. In order for anyone to make a delivery of copper, they basically had to buy it from Sumitomo. Prices skyrocketed, as copper sellers couldn't get the copper they needed to deliver – to Sumitomo – without first buying it at wildly inflated prices – from Sumitomo. Hamanaka was more than happy to oblige them, and his copper squeeze appeared to be a wild success.

The result is what's called a backwardation, a situation that means the spot price is trading higher than the forward price. Typically, the spot price is always lower than the forward price, which is normally called Contango. For example, if the spot price for copper was $1.10, the three-month forward price might be $1.15, which translates into a cost of five cents a pound to store the copper for three months.

But when there's no supply available for immediate delivery, the normal relationship reverses and it's called backwardation.

The term originated in the 19th century, and referred to a fee a buyer paid to delay the delivery of a commodity. Maybe shipments were delayed or there was a shortage of the goods; for some reason the commodity was in tight supply. Whatever the reason, the buyer wanted a delay and would ask the seller to wait for a short period of time and pay a backwardation fee. That fee was determined by the difference between the spot price and the forward price.

In commodities markets these days, the forward price is supposed to equal the spot price plus the cost of holding the commodity in a warehouse, the insurance, and any cost associated with financing it – just like the backwardation fees of yesteryear. Because of the cost associated with carrying commodities, backwardation should only happen during extreme circumstances. When it does, there's usually some kind of market dislocation. In the metals market, it usually means something like a miners strike, a shipping disruption, or, as in this case, some rogue trader owning almost 100% of the deliverable supply. Regardless, backwardations are usually short-lived.

There was a group of hedge funds which were keeping a very close eye on Hamanaka's activities, and they had been shorting copper for years. It was well-known throughout the industry that Hamanaka single-handedly controlled the market and speculation was rampant that he'd get caught any day. If that happened, the bottom would fall out and short-sellers stood to make a killing. But in order to go up against Hamanaka, you needed deep pockets. It would cost them in the short run, because Hamanaka was still hanging on.

Rumors began to swirl about a consortium of hedge funds who were collectively shorting copper in anticipation of Hamanaka's imminent demise. George Soros and Julian Robertson were both thought to be among them, as well as a bunch of European metals dealers.

Soros, however, bowed out before he could realize a profit; he was supposedly intimidated by Sumitomo's seemingly endless resources.

Because the LME is the benchmark for the world's copper price, the sudden jump in copper prices reverberated around the world. All of a sudden, there was a great economic incentive to get copper into LME warehouses. Copper in a LME warehouse was trading twelve cents per pound higher than the same copper sitting in a COMEX warehouse. As a result, COMEX traders began transporting physical copper from the COMEX warehouse in Arizona to the LME warehouse in Long Beach, California.

At the same time, there was a sudden surge in copper coming out of China. Chinese mining companies began selling more and more copper onto the world market, which was increasing the available supply. The same was true of other Asian countries, with copper pouring out of Taiwan, Korea, Japan, Malaysia, Thailand, and Indonesia. And because Hamanaka had accumulated so much, the sudden infusion coming out of the cracks could potentially ruin him.

As something of a stop-gap measure, Hamanaka moved hundreds of thousands of tons of copper out of the European LME warehouses and stashed them in non-LME warehouses in an attempt to make it look like the metal was disappearing. With impeccable timing, a Chinese government trading company took 100,000 tons of copper out of the market too, calling it a "national stockpile" and stored it in an unknown location. This action by the Chinese fueled rumors that Hamanaka was in cahoots with China's state-run metals trading company. Whether he was or not, the price of copper hit yet another record high.

Hamanaka seized the opportunity to sell some spot copper at astronomically high prices and rolled some of his long position into the forward contracts that were selling at lower prices. It is very likely that he planned to corner the market again three months later when those contracts came due.

YASUO HAMANAKA AND SUMITOMO, 1996

Hamanaka then amassed options to buy one million more metric tons of copper, though there were only 500,000 tons left in warehouses at the time. The price of copper shot up again. All told, at the beginning of 1996, Hamanaka controlled approximately $2 billion worth of copper, but his control was steadily loosening due to the rising copper mine production paired with decreasing demand in both Europe and Asia. He started to unload some of his holdings and prices kept going steadily downward.

Right then, it was clear that Hamanaka's efforts at the LME were affecting the U.S. copper market - copper supplies in the COMEX warehouses were at only 3,000 tons, down from an amount normally around 50,000 tons. That precipitous drop in supply would be the loophole that nailed Yasuo Hamanaka.

⋆   ⋆   ⋆

Because the LME was technically out of its jurisdiction, the United States Commodity Futures Trading Commission (CFTC) was unable to do anything about the market manipulation going on at the London exchange. For whatever reason, the U.K. regulators weren't as concerned. However, when the COMEX stockpiles had sunk to such ridiculously low levels and the price was so much lower in the U.S. than it was at the LME, the CFTC had the right to get involved because the U.S. market was being adversely affected.

In January of 1996, the CFTC began intensive discussions with British regulators visiting the United States. The topic of conversation was, naturally, Hamanaka and what he was doing to the world's copper markets. According to one CFTC official, representatives from the LME were stonewalling their American counterparts: "They didn't want us to know about the situation," he said after the meetings.

Not to be stymied by the LME, American regulators made direct contact with metals dealers in London to see if they could shed some light on what was happening across the pond. The London Securities and Investments Board (SIB) heard about the Americans' overtures and immediately cried foul. The British were resentful of U.S. officials trying to claim jurisdiction over their affairs. In an ironic twist that was inevitably lost on the British, one SIB official likened the Americans' actions to colonialism.

Irony and animosity aside, the SIB agreed to cooperate with the CFTC, as long as the CFTC agreed to route their inquiries through the SIB. In what came as a surprise to no one, SIB officials determined, after interviewing several metals traders, that Sumitomo was at the root of the market's odd behavior. Following the interviews, a British regulator contacted his regulatory counterpart in Japan and warned him that Sumitomo was facing big financial and regulatory problems.

The investigation culminated in April of 1996, when the CFTC – through their British colleagues – requested that Sumitomo make Yasuo Hamanaka available for questioning. Sumitomo agreed to the request and the firm reserved a room at the luxurious Waldorf-Astoria Hotel in Manhattan for their trader. The rationale was that the hotel was the only one that would allow Hamanaka to smoke in the hotel room. In addition to being a rogue trader, Hamanaka was also a chain smoker. It would be the last favor his firm did for him.

Early in May, the price of copper had already dropped down to $1.27 a pound, no doubt influenced by the events surrounding Hamanaka. It was, at that time, that information began to slowly percolate out of Sumitomo about the goings-on of Mr. Copper. Sumitomo claimed they received the first indication that there was a problem when they discovered a bank account with a $200,000 credit. Both the existence of the account itself and the money were news to Sumitomo's management.

By mid-May, it was widely assumed that Hamanaka had been fired from his job and, because he was no longer supporting the copper market, prices collapsed. Those short-sellers who had hung on were handsomely rewarded, as the price dipped to a just over 90 cents a pound. And then, the CFTC called Hamanaka back for a second round of questioning, this time set for June 5th.

Early that fateful day, Hamanaka learned that Merrill Lynch was about to announce the existence of his secret accounts and detail his activities. Perhaps in order to soften the blow, he immediately confessed to everything, going so far as to show how he "partially altered" reports. On June 12th, Sumitomo announced that Hamanaka had lost $1.8 billion and his employment was officially terminated. They were also quick to issue a statement in order to both distance themselves from the rogue trader casting themselves as victims, too: "These transactions were made solely by Yasuo Hamanaka himself. Hamanaka abused Sumitomo's name, and continued on with such unauthorized trading."

It is easy to be suspicious of such a statement. So many corporations have issued similar self-serving excuses about the activities of individuals. Sumitomo announced that they would set aside $1.4 billion to cover the losses and, very much to their credit, a portion of that amount - $110 million - would be taken from the pool of money that had been set aside to pay for executive bonuses. It's perhaps the first and only time that a company ever charged its own executives for the actions of a rogue trader.

The positions that Hamanaka had amassed weren't fully liquidated until September of that year, all the while Sumitomo's management was hoping that the price would rebound. They bet wrong, however, and the additional losses brought the total loss to $2.6 billion.

Then, on October 21, 1996, Tokyo police arrested Yasuo Hamanaka at his home in the suburb of Kawasaki. The event was covered by Japanese media, as an estimated twenty reporters camped out in front of his house that morning. During a search of the house, police found two letters with forged signatures, both dating back to 1994. It would take more than a month for Hamanaka to be indicted on fraud charges. He was going to stand trial for what he'd done.

Throughout the course of the investigation, which lasted more than a year, it was discovered that Hamanaka's attempts to manipulate copper weren't isolated events. He'd participated in and coordinated market squeezes in 1988, 1991, 1993 and 1995. It was also discovered that Sumitomo's risk management group was supposed to alert the head office if anyone exceeded their risk limits by more than $1 million. Obviously, in this case, that rule had been ignored. When Hiroshi Nishino, the company's Chief Risk Officer, was questioned in court, his standard response was "I have no memory of it."

Finally, on March 26, 1998, Yasuo Hamanaka pleaded guilty to four charges of forgery and fraud in Tokyo District Court. He was sentenced to eight years of hard labor, less the 400 days he'd already served since his arrest.

But Hamanaka wasn't the only one taking responsibility for his actions. It was determined that a variety of banks were complacent in helping him manipulate global copper prices. Sumitomo filed lawsuits totaling $2 billion against the banks who had assisted Hamanaka. Chase Manhattan paid $125 million to Sumitomo and $3.8 million in regulatory fines; Credit Lyonnais Rouse paid $310 million to Sumitomo and $10.8 million in fines; Merrill Lynch paid $275 to Sumitomo and $70 million in fines; UBS paid Sumitomo $250 million; Deutsche Sharps Pixley paid $2.5 million in fines; Rudolf Wolff paid $1.5 million in fines; and Morgan Stanley paid $1 million in fines. In the end, regulatory fines from the Hamanaka incident totaled $89.6 million, and damages paid to Sumitomo topped out at $985 million.

Lost in all of those numbers is the Global Minerals & Metals Corporation, which was the major player in the Hamanaka affair. They were eventually forced to pay $16 million in a class-action suit brought against them in civil court, which was a pittance compared to how much money they had made from Hamanaka. David Campbell points out that the $16 million was a "settlement" and not a "fine." They got lucky again when the CFTC, after an investigation, dismissed the case against them. "The case has consumed an unexpectedly large amount of time and resources, and will require a disproportionate share of resources for the foreseeable future," the commission's statement read. According to Campbell, "Did we affect spreads? Yes. But we kept it within the rules." For all of their involvement, GMMC would never face regulatory charges. Nothing. Nada.

In addition to going after the banks, Sumitomo also filed a civil charge against Hamanaka himself, as well as against Saburo Shimizu, but the results of those filings were never made public. Sumitomo was required to pay the UK's Financial Services Authority £5 million, and the CFTC $150 million, though they were allowed to do so "without admitting or denying any of the allegations." The fine was lower than it could have been because, the CFTC said, "Sumitomo management had provided substantial cooperation with the Commission in important respects," and noted that the firm had already "suffered significant losses." Moody's, however, wasn't quite as generous, as they downgraded Sumitomo's credit rating from A1 to A2.

*   *   *

Following the trial, metals trading volume moved into other metals and away from copper. Prices in the copper market plummeted after the incident, and within a year had plateaued around a price of about 95 cents a pound. With Hamanaka's departure from the market, speculators went elsewhere, with one trader remarking, "The sexy metals these days are zinc, nickel and aluminum."

By early 2000, that philosophy about "sexy metals" had been turned on its head once again. Worldwide demand for copper began to surge in what's referred to as the commodities super cycle. During a seven-year period, the price of copper went from a low of 60 cents a pound to a high of $3.50 a pound and China became the destination for over 40% of he world's copper production. These days, copper company executives are still expecting another bull market, as hybrid cars – which use nearly 100 pounds of copper per car – continue to grow in popularity. Investors seemed to agree with those executives, as the price of copper soared to yet a new record price in 2012 when it hit $4.2705 per pound, though it recently retreated back down to $3.00 in 2014.

It's still a fickle world inside the ring at the LME. The exchange still operates with the same open-outcry system and remains London's last trading pit to do so. Despite the ubiquitous nature of technology in other exchanges, there are no plans to do away with the system that the LME has used since its inception, despite the fact that the technology-laden Hong Kong Exchanges & Clearing, Ltd. purchased the LME in 2012.

Recently, there was a great deal of regulatory concern that banks were rigging the LME warehousing rules by creating deliberate bottlenecks by moving physical metals around for contract deliveries. When those bottlenecks appear, they directly affect the prices of the metals, and LME officials are very sensitive to that issue. There are also scattered reports of shadow warehouses, which are basically undocumented storage facilities utilized by hedge funds, merchants and banks. By moving metals from registered warehouses into shadow receptacles, groups are able to manipulate supplies, just like Hamanaka did back in 1996. The supply currently housed in these shadow warehouses is estimated to be much, much larger than what's in registered warehouses, and trading firms can profit off the knowledge of how much metal is moving between the two types of warehouses.

Traders are on-edge too, whenever there's even a whiff of an entity trying to corner the market; fear begins to run rampant. In November 2010, reports surfaced that one LME member held 50% of that exchange's copper, and by December the amount had grown to between 80% and 90%, which represented approximately $3 billion worth of copper. Stories spread throughout the market, and it was finally discovered that a trader at JP Morgan had accumulated a copper position equal to 80% of the LME warehouse supply, some of which was held in JP Morgan's own warehouses. Backwardation of the copper market ensued and the spot price jumped to $4.08 a pound versus the forward price of $3.94. The LME published a report detailing which firms held the open interest, and it was confirmed that JP Morgan's position was causing the backwardation.

JP Morgan had begun accumulating the copper that was stored in their own Henry Bath & Sons warehouse that was located in Baltimore, Maryland. Many of those involved in the market feared that they would again drive prices up, and that stockpiling created the panic that brought the whole issue to the forefront. Even though JP Morgan classified their copper purchases as passive investment, federal regulators were nevertheless alarmed.

In reality, the bank wasn't attempting to corner the market at all. Closer examination showed that JP Morgan's copper positions included their own proprietary holdings as well as those of their clients. The large position was because they were in the process of creating a copper Exchange Traded Fund (ETF). Even though there had been no malice aforethought on the part of the traders, the announcement that JP Morgan planned to create a copper ETF set off shockwaves. Investors are still easily spooked that there's another Yasuo Hamanaka lurking in the shadows.

In fact, regulators are so alarmed that the Federal Reserve is pressuring Wall Street banks to divest themselves of all commodity warehousing. Goldman Sachs and Morgan Stanley, in addition to JP Morgan, own metals warehouses, and both Goldman and Morgan Stanley have indicated their desire to keep those operations active. In short, the controversy brewing over banks' ownership of warehouses shows little sign of being resolved any time soon. JP Morgan announced plans to sell its Henry Bath & Sons warehouse to Swiss commodities firm Mercuria Energy Group. Only time will tell how the situation is resolved.

*   *   *

Yasuo Hamanaka – the man they once called "Mr. Copper" and "Mr. 5%" – was forty-eight years old when he was sentenced to prison. He was released in 2005, one year earlier than his original sentence had dictated. Upon his release, he commented to one reporter that he was "amazed" at how the price of copper had risen during his time in prison. But that was all he said. From there, he returned to the suburb of Kawasaki, presumably to live out the rest of his days in something resembling peace and quiet. Despite being only in his mid-fifties, his career was effectively over. The only life he'd ever known was that as a copper trader and there was no way a bank or metals trading firm was going to hire him. Most metals industry veterans don't believe Hamanaka was ever working for himself – he never had a personal trading account that was siphoning off profits. They believe he was strictly a company man, a Japanese "salaryman," always trying to make back the loss for the sake of Sumitomo. David Campbell went so far as to describe

Hamanaka as generally an "honest" man. Of course, if Hamanaka was innocent and honest, who was the real culprit?

Hamanaka continues to work, but now with his son, providing consulting services and introductions to important people in the scrap copper market, all the while, maintaining a very low profile in the business. As if to punctuate that fact, a reporter approached his house one day to get an interview with the disgraced trader and he was shooed away by Hamanaka's wife, who told him, "There's nothing to talk about."

THE NAB 4 AND NATIONAL AUSTRALIA BANK, 2004

By 2005, the four currency options traders who would become known as the NAB 4 were already facing trial in Australia. The head trader admitted directly in court, "I have fucked up and I have led a few people down the wrong path with me." He ended up pleading guilty to three charges and in exchange for leniency and his testimony against two of the others; those traders whom, by his own admission, he led down the wrong path. He received a 29-month prison sentence.

Those two traders pled not guilty to all of the charges against them - despite a mountain of evidence and paired with their boss's testimony – that proved their guilt. One was rewarded with three years and eight months in prison and the other found guilty on 12 different charges and sentenced to two years and four months. The last remaining member of the NAB 4 quartet, knowing that there was little-to-no hope of avoiding prison time, pled guilty to all charges and received a prison term of 16 months.

In somewhat of an ironic historical twist of fate, these four Australians would return to their native roots, serving prison sentences in the country that was originally established for that exact purpose.

*   *   *

Beginning with the Piracy Act of 1717, the country of Great Britain authorized itself to send its convicted criminals to its colonies. It was, at the time, the perfect solution to the main problem that plagued British prisons. They were overcrowded and in deplorable condition, and most of the prisoners died a miserable death while incarcerated. It made sense, then, to leverage this somewhat undesirable population to do something useful with their lives before they died. And the solution was to send them to the colonies; populating the new lands and spreading the British Empire around the globe.

Those who qualified for "transportation" – as it was officially called - were those convicted of crimes not severe enough to warrant the death penalty. The sentences ranged from several years for crimes such as larceny or robbery, to longer sentences for things like mutiny, desertion, or insubordination for military personnel. Many convicts were merely guilty of poaching game animals from a lord's property. In the event a criminal was transported for a sentence shorter than life, that convict was responsible for his or her own transportation back to Britain, if that was, in fact, something the ex-convict still wanted.

The convicted felons were initially ferried across the pond to America, resulting in as many as 120,000 being transported over the years. Once the shot heard 'round the world' triggered the dawn of the American Revolution in 1776, the penal shipments came to an abrupt end, never to resume. It created a problem for the British, as there were still plenty of eligible convicts available each year for transportation, and, all of a sudden, there was an immediate need for a new destination to serve as a penal colony.

Enter Australia.

Beginning in 1770, Great Britain claimed the eastern half of Australia as a colony, which seemed perfectly suited as the new penal destination, despite the fact that it was situated more than 10,000 miles away. So, on January 26, 1788, the First Fleet arrived in what was then called Port Jackson, or Sydney Harbor, as it is known today. The fleet carried 252 British Marines and their families, as well as a total of 751 convicts (together with their families) who had been sentenced to serve the time in the New South Wales penal colony.

By the time England ceased transportation to the Australian colonies in 1868, they had established four main settlements – Norfolk Island, Van Diemen's Land (modern-day Tasmania), and Moreton Bay, along with the original colony of New South Wales – and Australia became the home to an estimated 162,000 displaced British citizens.

Most modern-day Australians are descended from those who were shipped Down Under, but today's Australia is a very different world from the one their ancestors first encountered. By the beginning of the twenty-first century, Australia was no longer the recipient criminals from distant lands, but at the forefront of the cutting-edge financial markets and the transportation of money around the globe. The Foreign Exchange Market – simply forex or FX – was a booming business in Australia, with the buying and selling of currencies happening in fractions of a second. But those criminal roots ran deep, at least for some traders, and a group that came to be known as the NAB 4 carried on what can only be called a family tradition.

*   *   *

The NAB 4 practiced their trade at National Australia Bank, which was originally established in 1858 as the National Bank of Australasia, a name taken from the geographical term coined in 1756 to refer to the collective of Australia, New Zealand, New Guinea and the neighboring islands. Set up by Alexander Gibb and Andrew Cruickshank during the Australian gold rush, the bank primarily financed payments for Australian exports of wool, gold and other commodities bound for London.

In 1893, the bank changed its name to National Bank Limited and eventually merged with the Commercial Banking Company of Sydney Limited in 1981, with the combined entity called the National Australia Bank (NAB). NAB bought the Bank of New Zealand in 1992, and today is the largest bank in Australia, with 1808 branches in operation and nicknamed "The National" by the Aussies.

One of the more lucrative divisions of NAB was the Commercial and Investment Bank (CIB), which employed approximately 2,600 people and generated in excess of A$1 billion annually in pre-tax profits. Of that amount, half of those profits were generated by the 550 traders in the Markets Division, which included money markets, commodities, derivative products and foreign exchange trading. This group was responsible for both making-markets for the bank's customers and proprietary trading on behalf of the bank itself. Drilling further down in the Markets Division was the NAB foreign exchange trading group, which had trading desks in Melbourne, London and New York City, and sales desks in Sydney, Wellington, Singapore and Hong Kong.

The main dealing room – the epicenter of the bank's financial markets business – was housed on the 32nd floor, located at 500 Bourke Street in Melbourne. The dealers who populated this floor were widely known as major players in both the Australian and New Zealand markets, and they considered themselves very, very good at their jobs. Gary Dillon, who was the Global Head of Foreign Exchange at NAB, even boasted of the business, "I believe the NAB currency options business...is far superior to others in the market and to most others internally." That is, at least The National thought they had a top notch trading operation.

Despite that glowing praise heaped on them by Dillon, the traders didn't believed that their boss was "far superior" in anyway. They called him slow to act and incapable of making decisions. There was constantly a tangible tension in the relationship between Dillon and the currency traders, but the currency options division was his baby. He'd started it at NAB and built it into a major force in the market, an accomplishment that was due in no small part to the people he hired.

Dillon was recruited directly by NAB in July of 1998. His mandate was to develop and lead a foreign exchange trading and market-making business. Dillon, in turn, first recruited a young and egotistical hot-shot named Luke Duffy to head the newly-formed FX options desk. Duffy was not shy when it came to his own self-worth or that of the desk he ran. He was personally convinced that they were the best in the world, even going so far as to refer to his desk as the BOAT – the "Biggest of All Time." He ran the FX options desk as his own personal fiefdom, and didn't like anyone crossing him in any kind of way; even referring to traders who left his desk for other jobs as "Judases." With that, he maintained a blacklist of traders who had crossed him at one time or another. He also had a penchant for assigning nicknames.

"Pill Boy" was assigned to David Bullen, a name Bullen inherited due to his appreciation of illicit pharmaceuticals. His nickname was later changed to "Buddha Boy," but that's something we'll get into later. Bullen was just one year younger than his boss and began at NAB in 1993 after graduating from Monash University. He bounced around from one trading desk to another for a few years at The National before accepting a position with another bank in Singapore. After two years without Bullen, NAB decided that they wanted him back and, in February 2002, he rejoined NAB as a senior dealer in currency options.

Vince Ficarra was the youngest on the desk, at a mere 23 years when he joined forces with Dillon in 2000 as a junior trader. His friends called him Vinnie, though Dillon took to calling him "Rat," due to the young man's persistent questioning of the Dillon's trading strategies.

Gianni Gray had started in the London office in 1998, moved to Melbourne in July of 2000, then boomeranged back to London in 2003. Dillon zeroed-in on Gray's own personal values when it came time to dish out names. Gray was uncomfortable with trader culture and found the constant jokes to be somewhat distasteful. Clearly he didn't fit in the rough and tumble trading floor of the National. That personal sentiment earned him the names of "G-Spot" and "Square."

*   *   *

The currency markets exploded in the mid-1970s after the Bretton Woods Agreement was abruptly cancelled by the United States in 1971. Previously, the value of every major world currency was fixed to the U.S. Dollar, and the Dollar itself was fixed to the price of gold. Before the 1970s, there was little fun trading foreign exchange – given that the exchange rates were fixed and rarely moved. But after Bretton Woods fell apart, currency prices floating freely and a whole new trading market popped up overnight at banks around the world, becoming a worldwide decentralized over-the-counter market. For any company transporting goods to far away lands, it allowed businesses to convert one currency into another one. For money managers investing abroad, it allowed them to hedge against a country's currency increasing or decreasing in value. So, enter the need for banks to offer foreign exchange services. By 1977, there was $18 billion traded in the global FX market every day. By 2004, that number had ballooned to $1.2 trillion, becoming one of the largest financial markets in the world, along with several sub-markets, like currency options.

Foreign exchange trades are done in pairs, meaning there are always two currencies involved in any transaction. For example, buying the USD/AUD means someone is buying U.S. dollars and selling Australian dollars (A$). Buying the NZD/AUD means buying the New Zealand dollar and selling the Australian dollar. The FX options desk at NAB traded a total of 43 different currency pairs, but specifically concentrated on combinations of five different currencies: U.S. dollars, Euros, Australian dollars, New Zealand dollars (known as Kiwis to the traders), and the British Pound Sterling.

Typical trading in the FX market is divided into two different categories: spot and forwards. FX forwards, are simply the forward – or the future – settlement of an exchange of currencies. In the spot market – historically known as "trading on the spot" – currencies are traded for immediate settlement. Whereas, forwards take into account the cost to borrow one currency and lending the other for that period of time. For example, if an FX forward contract settles 90 days in the future, the three-month interest rate for each currency affects the forward price. The spot price of the exchange rate, the interest rate to borrow one currency and the interest rate to lend the other currency all determine the forward price. At the National, the FX spot desk was a separate trading unit, and the FX options desk was required to execute any FX spot transactions through them. Like at any trading floor, it created tension between the two desks.

Due to the global nature of the business, there's constant FX trading at all hours of the day, around-the-clock, with traders working in various shifts to cover the specific time zones. In the case of a large bank, they will frequently have FX desks in

Asia, Europe and the United States, with traders passing the trading book from one time zone to the next. In the case of NAB's Melbourne office, if a trader was assigned the London shift, it meant working from 5:00 PM to 12:00 AM in Melbourne time. The most dreaded shift, however, was the New York shift, which ran from midnight until 7:00 in the morning. The NAB traders took turns on this one, and clearly nobody wanted it.

There is an old saying that you learn your risk tolerance by investing in the stock market. It's essentially a warning to timid investors. If losses scare you, it's best to stick to the most passive investments. The drawback about staying away from speculative investments is that greater risk is typically associated with greater reward. So the more you're willing to take risk, the more you can potentially gain. And that's where options trading comes in. There, market volatility and risk taking are the name of the game.

As far as Luke Duffy, "Pill Boy," "Rat," and "Square" were concerned, their action centered around currency options, and the market volatility which drove the prices of those options. Just like other options markets, FX options traders are buying and selling the right, as opposed to the obligation, to buy or sell a currency at a given price by some pre-set date in the future. The two types of options are broken down into calls and puts. A call option gives someone the right to buy a currency at a set price; a put gives them the right to sell it.

Then, the permutations of buying and selling calls and puts create a variety of ways to play the market. If you own a call option, you are looking for the exchange rate to rise; that is, you're expecting the price of one currency to increase relative to the price of another. If you buy a put option, you're expecting the exchange rate to decline. But you can also sell calls and sell puts. That way, you can bet on a declining market by selling a call and bet on a rising market by selling a put – just the opposite of buying the options.

In theory, it means that buying a call and selling a put are about the same thing – you're betting on a rising market. Just like buying a put and selling a call is betting on a declining market. But there's an important difference. When you're buying the option, you're paying a premium to have a right. With it, you have a very limited risk if the market goes against you. The most you can lose is the premium, or the price you paid for the option. When selling an option, things become a little more dicey. You have to consider that selling someone an option they gives *them* unlimited upside if the market goes their way.

Because the seller is giving the buyer unlimited upside, options prices are driven by the volatility of the market; that's how much exchange rates are moving up and down each day. Suppose that the Australian dollar is trading against the U.S. dollar at an exchange rate of 1.51. That is, someone can buy 1.51 Australian dollars for every U.S. dollar they sell on the spot forex market. An investor who believes that value of the U.S. dollar is going to increase in value, say they expect the exchange rate to move past 1.60, might buy a 3-month call option to buy the U.S. dollar at 1.60 (AUD/USD). That gives the buyer the right to buy the U.S. dollar for 1.60 Australian dollars at any time before the option contract expires in ninety days. If the spot exchange rate goes above 1.60, the call option is said to be "in the money," and the owner of the buyer can exercise the option to buy U.S. dollars and sell Australian dollars at a profit.

Now, let's say the underlying currency isn't fluctuating very much – say the exchange rate trades between 1.51 to 1.52 throughout the average trading day – then there's little chance of reaching the strike price of 1.60. It might not be such a smart trading idea to buy that option, then again, the price of the option won't cost too much because the market's volatility is so low. So the option can have a lot of potential upside in the unlikely event it ever hits the strike price.

Now, suppose the currency is trading much more actively, that is, there's more volatility in the market. Let's say it's trading between 1.51 and 1.58 each day. At that point, the chances are much greater that it might trade above 1.60. Remember, selling options carries with it a huge amount of risk. There is virtually unlimited downside for the options seller, so the larger the trading range of a given currency, the more likely it could trade above the option's strike price. In other words, the greater the volatility, the greater the chances that the seller will be required to make good on the option.

There's another important factor to take into account, and that's how long before the option expires, or the time value of the option. Again, the longer the owner has to exercise the option, the better the chance of the exchange rate passing the strike price of 1.60. A six-month option would have more time value than a one-week option – a lot can happen in six months that probably won't happen in a week. There's just not as good of a chance the option will pass the strike price in a week to become in-the-money.

That's why traders buy and sell options based on the volatility of the market. Specifically, when market volatility is considered too high, traders often sell options. With the risk inherent in selling the option comes an immediate – and guaranteed – reward: the large premium they receive. That's cash in hand for the seller, and as every day passes and the currency hasn't traded past the strike price, there is a progressively lower likelihood that the option will go from being out-of-the-money to in-the-money. As the chances grow slimmer, the option's price drops, too.

The National's FX options trading desk was holding between 800 to 3,000 different options at any one time. Long calls, short calls, long puts and short puts on any variety of different strike prices in all of the combinations of currency pairs. Their official stated trading strategy was to "sell low delta options against buying high delta options for the cheaper volatility." In other words, they sold options that were way out-of-the-money (far away from the 1.60 strike price) and bought options that were closer to being in-the-money (close to the 1.60 strike price). They were good at taking risk in an incredibly volatile – and very lucrative – market. In calm FX markets they generally made a lot of money, but they were constantly risking a lot of money if the market moved too far and too fast. They called themselves the BOAT, The Biggest Of All Time, and clearly felt confortable trading the market. Throughout the history of the foreign exchange market, big moves made many fortunes for many in the FX market, but it's those same moves caused financial destruction for the not-so-lucky. Or, as in the case of the NAB 4, the financial destruction of those who took losses and tried to hide them. We've seen it all so many times before.

*   *   *

Within the confines of The National's trading floor, the environment was one of aggressive male domination, to say the least. It was particularly appropriate over at the FX options trading desk. The traders were seen around the bank as especially aggressive – even in the already aggressive environment of the National – and they were as arrogant as they were aggressive. The majority of their interaction was only with one another, as nobody else at the bank wanted to approach them unless they had to. The traders even assigned derogatory nicknames for those whom they worked with, as if to establish a caste system with the traders themselves firmly planted at the top. Jubs were those who served in support capacities in the operations and the back office. They were, in the traders' minds, people who had a job, but didn't know what they were doing. The London Stench Boys were the FX spot traders, who were segregated from the FX options desk. And those who worked too hard for the bank were Nabbas, or people who had officially sold their souls to the bank.

Yes, the FX options traders were arrogant and unpleasant, but at the end of the day, the only thing that truly mattered was that they were making money. The NAB philosophy was that anything goes in the pursuit of profits. It didn't matter what a trader was doing, so long as he was bringing in the dough. And that philosophy across the trading floor would have disastrous consequences.

Risk limits at The National were, it seems, something of a guideline, at least in the minds of those charged with enforcing them. "Management would normally exercise some control," David Bullen would later recall, "but it seemed that, as we were making money...we were pretty much left to our own devices with minimal interference." Indeed, a 2001 internal audit review of the FX options trading desk revealed that on 61 different days during the trading year, the traders had exceeded their risk limits. What's more, the Global Head of Foreign Exchange had approved every instance of excessive risk-taking, with no questions asked.

Taking risk was something of a drug for the traders. Oftentimes when the market was slow and there wasn't much activity, they'd appease their addiction by gambling on Internet game sites. With minimal oversight, the culture at the bank – and again, especially for the FX options traders – was one of non-adherence to management and limits. In a statement issued after the dust had settled following the discovery of the NAB 4's nefarious activities, PriceWaterhouseCoopers would say, "We believe the culture...is highly relevant to an understanding of what went wrong."

Don't get the impression that life at NAB was all work and no play; that's pretty important to understanding the overall culture in which the traders were operating. Entertainment was a big part of the game, and their brokers provided them with what can only be referred to as the high life. On one outing, when their brokers rolled into town from Tokyo and Singapore in November of 2000, the NAB 4 group was invited to the famous Flemington Racecourse in Melbourne. Duffy, Pill Boy, Rat, and Square were all treated to a marquee tent in the infield, with all of them – together with their wives and girlfriends – flown in by helicopter. David Bullen said of the affair, "I felt a bit like a rock star, and I planned to act like one as well." Following the day's racing, the group headed off to the docklands area to a nightclub called Perfecto, where they danced until the wee hours of the morning, with plenty of ecstasy tablets being passed around all night.

The club scene was Bullen's weaknesses. He loved going out late, which accustomed him to staying up all night, a fact that came in handy when it was his turn to work the New York shift. He had a special love for the techno music that blasted in the clubs; "I had a date with the techno music that I loved so much and the drug ecstasy," he said of a night's activities. And while he "found ecstasy awesome," Bullen's true drug of choice was speed. "I had never come across a better drug than speed," he said. "I recognized my own weakness, and taking drugs was it at the moment. There was no point in fighting it."

It is telling that Bullen admitted to recognizing his own weakness, but equally telling that he limited that weakness to taking drugs. It was his failure to recognize – or at least to acknowledge – his other weaknesses, specifically his penchant for risk-taking and his own immense ego, that would lead to his personal destruction.

*   *   *

The seeds of their eventual downfall were sewn, quite by accident, in 2001. Vanessa McCallum, the FX options trading assistant, accidentally entered a trade incorrectly. The mistake created a false loss of A$1 million; an error that remained in their new trade processing system named Horizon for more than a week before the traders on the desk caught it and corrected it.

Up until 1999, the traders at The National used a trade processing system called Devon. It had served the bank well for many years, but as the markets become more complicated, more technical, and mathematically based, the Devon trade processing system became insufficient and outdated. The trading desk set out to create a new trading system, and wanted it custom designed to fit their own standards, so they hired an outside IT development group to create it. The new system – called Horizon – was installed in 2000.

The Horizon system was used to monitor their profits and losses, as well as to book their trades. Among the new features and improvements was the streamlining of the processes between the front office, back office, and accounting areas. Most importantly, especially to the guys on the desks, the new system contained an valuation model that priced the options, including the volatilities implied by the strike prices which traders called the smile.

Surprisingly, however, nobody in the back office noticed the A$1 million loss. When Luke Duffy complained to the Jubs, whose job it was to notice such things, the reply came back that it wasn't their responsibility to check the accuracy of internal trades. Internal trades are those trades that are booked from one internal source to another, such as trader-to-trader, office-to-office or department-to-department. All of the trades that take place entirely within the bank. That succinct passing-of-the buck unknowingly created the perfect blueprint for a financial scam.

*   *   *

The idea began to morph into reality in 2001. Bullen was at a bar called Irish Times when he received a call from Gianni Gray. In a surprise move on the FX market, they lost about A$1 million in the space of a couple of hours. The trading desk's collective ego didn't want declare the loss outright, and memories of that internal trade oversight spawned the idea to cover it up. The group naturally assumed they could make it back if they played their cards right, so they decided to cover up their flub. They put through a spot FX trade with another trading desk – marking it as an internal trade – at the wrong exchange rate. And with that, the million-dollar loss ceased to exist anywhere on the bank's ledgers.

The loss still existed, of course, and luckily the group managed to trade their way to a profit of between A$6 million and A$8 million during the next couple of months. That gain wasn't enough to fully make their budget for the year, though; by the end of September 2001, they were back carrying losses totaling approximately A$4 million for the year. But those losses were again easy enough to wipe out, at least from the prying eyes within the bank. All they had to do was put through a single internal trade that showed a A$4 million gain and – POOF – the loss was suddenly cloaked from sight. As far as the accounting system was concerned, the desk was mildly profitable for the fiscal year, which ended September 30, 2001. Betting one's career that no one was checking internal trades could work well for a little while, but it was nothing they could count on for the long term. They'd gotten away with it this time; next time they might not be so lucky.

Not surprisingly, the traders began to take a great interest in the inner workings of the back office. Obviously, if you're hiding multi-million dollar losses, you're bound to be pretty interested in how the system works. After all, the better you know the system, the easier it is to locate and exploit the weaknesses. So the traders began having lengthy discussions with the Jubs about how the settlement system worked. Of course, many of these discussions centered on the reconciliation processes undertaken by the back-office staff and how their trades were checked and verified. All the time, the Jubs were providing the traders with very important information about how things worked on their end. The traders were clearly taking, in hindsight, a far greater interest in the back-office than typical traders.

The trading desk found they could also disguise their losses by rigging their mark-to-market (MTM) prices. At any bank, trading positions are supposed to be valued at their current market at the end of the day. If a trader, for example, had bought U.S. dollars and sold 1.51 Australian dollars against it, the initial price of the trade was 1.51 AUD/USD. If the U.S. dollar went up to 1.52 to the Aussie, the end-of-day MTM price should be 1.52, even though the trader hasn't yet sold their U.S. dollars and bought back the Aussie dollars. In this case, the trader made one point that day. Pretty straightforward. But when it came time to value between 800 and 3,000 different currency options trades at the end of the day, the process became a little more complicated. And complexity often opens the door to manipulation.

At the National's FX options desk, traders used external prices they obtained from their brokers to establish the volatilities and price some of the options they were trading. The more exotic options were illiquid, which meant that their actual prices were difficult to determine and not readily available. Picture some way-out-of-the-money options on the Aussie/Kiwi exchange rate. Only someone with direct access to the specific market knew where those options were trading and the volatilities. In those cases, the trading desk was simply allowed to apply their own MTM prices, a practice that fulfilled the requirement of having the positions marked, but opened the door for collusion with their brokers. One options trader would choose the MTM price and send it to the broker. The broker, in turn, copied the information into a new email and sent it back to them unchanged. No challenges, no discussion, no anything. The bank's risk management crew thought they were getting good, independent prices; all the while they got whatever the traders wanted them to get.

They rationalized hiding the losses pretty easily. Because NAB's management didn't like large swings in profit and loss – the larger the swings indicated they were taking more risk – they decided what they were doing was just smoothing out their numbers. That meant, in basic terms, adjusting both their profits and their losses a little lower. It gave a comforting feeling to bank management that the desk was keeping their risk-taking under control. The main smoother on the desk was Gianni Gray, a job assigned to him by his boss Luke Duffy; though the job was undertaken by every-one at one time or another. It was, in their collective minds, a great way to justify hiding their losses. They were just doing what the bank wanted them to do, namely, smoothing their profits and losses to fit the bank's risk profile.

It might seem somewhat odd that they could have gotten away with the smoothing activities, but again, the oversight was minimal. Management simply reviewed the end-of-day reports and nothing more. It seemed that everyone outside of the bank knew about the problems at NAB's FX options desk except the people who were supposed to know about them. The sentiment was echoed by an FX options trader at another bank, "I can tell you that NAB traders have been doing dodgy trading for much longer than a few months. The global options market has been waiting for them to blow up for years."

Inputting false internal trades and adjusting the MTM prices on exotic options positions was one thing, but, eventually someone - the bank's accounting system, auditors or risk managers – were going to catch on to them. At least that's what should have happened. The problem here was that they still had an ace in the hole, something else they discovered from the detailed discussions with the back-office staff. Those discussions opened up an even easier way to hide their losses.

There were two different trade processing systems at the bank. Horizon was used to process their trades internally, while another system called Kapiti was responsible for reconciling the trades done with other banks. Any time there are two separate banks agreeing on trades, there can be mistakes made on the details of the trade. Kapiti was the system to reconcile those trades between the banks. And in that reconciliation process, perhaps not surprisingly, the traders found another loophole.

Horizon was programmed to close down for its end-of-day at 8:00 AM Melbourne time, which was 3:00 PM in New York - the designated hour for close-of-business for the global foreign exchange market. Once Horizon had completed its end-of-day run, it would shutdown and restart for the next day's operations. At that point, the back-office would begin to confirm the trades from the day before. That is not out-of-the-ordinary for a trading system. But again, when you've got two separate systems working in tandem, there's a gap between them. And in the case of Horizon and Kapiti, that gap was a big one. As big as two hours, in fact.

Kapiti didn't typically start up until between 8:15 AM and 10:00 AM Melbourne time. So there was a period of time anywhere from 15 minutes up to two hours between the time when Horizon ended its trading day and Kapiti began the reconciling of trades from the day before. So right before Horizon shut down at 8:00 AM, the traders were free to input trades at off-market prices. Then, once Horizon was restarted, they could delete their off-market trades from the system. No one could detect the false trades because they vanished before they were confirmed with other banks. Using this method, the traders could book whatever trades they wanted at whatever prices they wanted, and without detection. The reports that were checked by accounting and risk management included the false trades. There was no way to catch the false trades because they disappeared before they were confirmed with the other banks.

Duffy, Bullen, Ficarra, and Gray successfully gamed the system this way beginning in 2001. They could trade anyway they wanted. If they took a loss, the only thing they had to do was input trades at the off-market prices before 8:00 AM then simply and cancel them a few minutes later. Nobody else knew about the flaw in the system, but nobody was looking for one either. The FX options traders had their fool-proof way to hide their losses.

Keep in mind that the daily booking of false trades created a situation where they needed to keep one step ahead of management, risk management and bank auditors. Someone had to be there to book the trades each morning. They couldn't miss a day or their fraud would come to light.

By the beginning of 2002, Bullen and Gray had become the A-Team on the desk, being responsible for all trades involving AUD/USD, EUR/USD, GBP/USD and EUR/GBP, and their collective budget for 2002 was set at A$5 million. But while their game of hide-and-seek with losses continued undetected, other banks weren't taking quite such a laissez-faire attitude with them in the market.

In March of that year, another Australian bank publicly raised concerns regarding the NAB options desk, and forwarded those concerns to the National's management. In response, NAB sent a team of senior officials to discuss the matter in person. Following that meeting, management passed over the concerns, determining that the other bank didn't fully understand exactly what their options desk was doing. Clearly the National's team was the BOAT, other banks just didn't understand the complexities associated with NAB's proprietary trading techniques.

But while the upper-level folks ignored the concerns, Duff, Bullen, Ficarra and Gray did the exact opposite. They made it very clear to their brokers that if any bank raised concerns about them, NAB would cut them off from any future FX business. To add to the threat, the traders told the brokers in no uncertain terms that if the brokers continued to spread rumors, they'd be cut them off too. It was, at its core, an obvious case of financial blackmail. The message was essentially one of, "If we hear about anyone criticizing us, you'll pay." And just like in the movies, the traders' threats worked.

In May of 2002, however, an interesting incident involving a rogue trader in the currency markets hit the headlines. John Rusnak, the head FX trader in Allied Irish Bank's trading operation in the U.S., had tried to disguise his own mammoth losses by selling options. The FX market had moved against him and when the dust had settled, Rusnak had lost approximately $750 million.

That incident caught the attention of NAB's management and their Board of Directors, who collectively discussed the matter at great length. In the minutes from that meeting, it is clear that while recognizing the hazards, the directors felt they were doing everything correctly: "A report concerning Allied Irish Bank's FX losses had been reviewed," the minutes read, and it was even noted that National Australia Bank "had appropriate controls in place to identify control breakdowns on a timely basis to ensure that any FX losses are minimized." In reality, they really didn't.

The noose around the necks of the NAB 4 should have been tightening, but it wasn't. A rogue trading event had occurred under very similar circumstances, but NAB officials took little action to investigate their own FX options trading business. There was no action to make sure that their traders were acting properly, nor was there any strengthening of the existing risk management procedures. Of course, hindsight is 20/20, so it's hard to blame them for their lack of initiative. Everything remained status quo, and it was just what the traders wanted.

The pressure of mounting losses was beginning to weight on the traders. Bullen decided to make some personal changes in his own life. He had no problem with continuing his illegal trading activities, to be sure, but there was a noticeable change in the party boy's lifestyle. He changed his diet to that of a raw-food vegetarian, claiming that "diseases result from cooking our food and killing enzymes in the process, and from consuming animal products." He also gave up all dairy products, claiming that they were a leading cause of cancer in humans. The trader formerly known as Pill Boy gave up his clubbing lifestyle, too, going so far as to skip the broker outings and entertainment that went along with trading. "My day-to-day life was becoming simpler," he said of the change. "I really didn't care too much about the job."

Bullen had given up all socializing with friends and colleagues and, perhaps most out-of-character for a high-flying currency trader, he began studying the works of Zen masters and the teachings of Buddha. He said of his conversion, "extreme bliss was present in me every day." That change led to a new moniker for Pill Boy. Following his new-found inner peace, the boys at work began calling him Buddha Boy.

He would later say about the desk, "We seem to share a mutual delusion that we should chase money. We kill for it, lie and cheat for it, and sell our bodies for it." But despite his philosophical awakening, Bullen was still a money guy at his core.

By the end of their fiscal year in September 2002, Buddha Boy and his cohorts were in the unenviable position of carrying a whopping A$8 million loss, an amount they had concealed throughout the year by inputting and deleting trades each morning. When the year ended, their meager profits weren't enough for everyone on the desk to get a bonus, and Bullen was left out in the cold when it came time to hand out the checks. After that, he seriously considered leaving NAB for another bank.

But Bullen decided to stay around for another year, and with the flipping of the fiscal calendar to 2003, the desk was given a new budget of a whopping A$37 million. With what appeared to be a clean slate, the team set out to make that huge number for the year, and it only took the first month to get off to a rocky start. In October 2002, Bullen and Gray took a huge hit when some EUR/USD options moved against them, costing the pair a cool A$1 million on a single trade. It was, they reasoned, all because they were in Melbourne, working inhuman hours to trade the U.S. dollar market which mostly traded in London and New York. They decided that one of them needed to move to London to be nearer the action and Gray took the assignment.

Compounding the problems was the fact that they were also sustaining heavy losses in the USD/JPY trading book; a book that had been transferred to them by another trading desk. Dillon wasn't happy about it, to say the least, and called Bullen into his office for a reckoning. One of the last things a trader ever wants is a lashing from his boss's boss. Dillon asked point-blank why the book was down A$5 million and all Bullen could do was promise to do better.

By the spring of 2003, the desk was down between A$3 million and A$6 million, not to mention the fact that they were still a long way from achieving their budget of A$37 million. But as the fourth quarter dawned in July, lightning struck. The desk was heavily short AUD/USD options, and the Australian dollar dropped signif- icantly. They had made back their entire A$5 million loss which put them flat for the year. Flat was okay, but not great. And it certainly wasn't enough to generate the kind of bonuses they wanted. They needed something big. Something to clean up their books and shoot them past their budgeted number. They needed a big trade and a big market move. And soon.

As September rolled around, they were betting heavily that both the Australian and New Zealand dollars would drop in value against the U.S. dollar. They were making money again and were up a modest A$8.9 million. They had a big short of $210 million in a variety of currencies, including the Australian and New Zealand dollars against being long $218 million U.S. dollars.

The background that drove them hinged on the G-7 meeting that was about to begin. The Group of Seven or G-7 was, essentially, a governing body charged with preserving global economic stability. It was composed of the finance ministers from the seven largest economies in the world: the United States, the United Kingdom, France, Germany, Italy, Canada and Japan. Ahead of the meeting, the traders expected the group to promote a policy of tightly-managed exchange rates, which would translate into heavier volatility in both the Australian and New Zealand dollars, as well as a corresponding strengthening of the U.S. dollar. If the ministers agreed to the expected policy, NAB's trading book would make a lot of money and they would easily make their budget for the year.

In fact, the desk was so sure that the G-7 would push for tighter exchange rates that they increased their long position in U.S. dollars to $271 million by buying a variety of options. They were long all kinds of out-of-the-money and at-the-money options, including butterfly spreads that combined both long at-the-money options and short out-of-the-money options. In short, they were making a huge play that market volatility would subside in the U.S. dollar and increase in the Aussie and Kiwi dollars.

On September 21, 2003, the day before the G-7 meeting, there was strong intervention by many central banks in their respective currencies. Both Japan and China were active in the market, aggressive buying and selling U.S. dollars and Euros. When the group met the following day, it ended with an announcement supporting "more flexibility in exchange rates," a comment that market players saw as a major shift in policy. It sent the U.S. dollar plummeting, as it immediately lost 150 basis points, or 1.5%. Bullen recalled that "volatilities erupted" following the announcement and "the one-month [volatility] went from around eight-percent to over sixteen-percent in a couple of days."

The drop in the U.S. dollar was compounded by a sustained and significant rally in both the Australian and New Zealand dollars. Just the opposite of what they were banking on, and now, the National's traders were rapidly losing money on both sides of their bet. Had they immediately closed out the positions, the losses could have been manageable, but then again, the group had the ability to easily hide their losses. There was always an easy "out" to hide losses and now it was just a part of how they did business. No reason to cover losses, they reasoned, they'd make them back at some point.

Within days, the U.S. dollar was down a full four cents against the Australian dollar. With the U.S. dollar in free-fall, NAB became progressively shorter and shorter - the Aussie and Kiwi options they were short were progressively moving from out-of-the-money to in-the-money. It added to their mounting losses. And those losses came fast and furious. On each of three days – September 19, September 22 and September 26 – they were down another A$5 million each day. But despite that, they adjusted the internal system to still show, unbelievably, a profit of A$1.8 million.

By the end of September, their losses had mushroomed, erasing all the meager profits they'd made over the past month, destroyed by a A$42 million loss during the final week of September. But then again, all they had to do was rig the system to show a year-end profit totaling A$37 million, which was exactly what they did. And, on top of that, it was enough for them to get their year-end bonuses. When it came time to hand-out the congratulations, Duffy joked that he planned to go into the meeting and say, "G'day, guys! We had a great year. Pay us loads of money!" Ficarra opined that he'd be happy with A$100,000 because, as he said, "I'm only twenty-five – only turned twenty-five a month ago – and a bonus of A$100,000 is a lot of money for me!" They all had pretty big expectations.

In the end, despite a hidden loss of A$42 million, each of the four FX options traders received nice bonuses. Duffy pocketed A$265,000; Bullen A$215,000; Gray A$190,000; and the only-twenty-five-a-month-ago Ficarra took home A$120,000. They were all pretty pleased.

Despite their bonuses, the deception began taking its toll on the traders themselves. Ficarra would admit in a taped phone conversation with Duffy, "It's always real hard doing this shit." Duffy asked him why he felt that way, to which Ficarra replied, "Basically it involves telling lies, which I guess I can do. I'm impartial to telling lies." Bullen, in line with his new Buddhist lifestyle, was slightly more philosophical on the subject: "I hated this part of the job – when you knew you were walking into losses and there wasn't a thing you could do about it."

*   *   *

Famed author Ray Bradbury, who was best known for his work *Fahrenheit 451*, once wrote, "He had never liked October. Ever since he had first lay in the autumn leaves before his grandmother's house many years ago and heard the wind and saw the empty trees. It had made him cry, without a reason. And a little of that sadness returned each year to him. It always went away with spring. But it was a little different tonight. There was a feeling of autumn coming to last a million years. There would be no spring." Those words, poetic as they are, were an apt description for the beginning of the 2004 fiscal year at the National. As October began, the hole they had created was growing ever deeper, and there was nothing they could do but keep digging. Over the next four months, the slide in the market continued. The U.S. dollar dropped 8% overall, including an 11% drop against the Euro.

Their shovel in October came in the form of an inter-office memo from the National's back office. Due to cost-cutting measures, "The currency options back office does not check internal deals. At least in the short term, this situation will not change." Reinforcing their original method of hiding losses. That change, was essentially a public announcement that traders suddenly had an unchecked way of hiding their losses that way again.

At first, the announcement was taken as a Heaven-sent gift for Luke Duffy. The traders were now able to enter one-sided trades with an internal account at off-market prices to generate false profits. It was clear, nobody was looking over their shoulders to make sure their trades were accurate. It meant they could now input options trades with longer expiration dates and leave them there, which, in turn, meant that they no longer had to worry about booking false trades and cancelling them each morning. In addition to making their collective deception easier, the change came at a perfect time for the NAB 4, as it was growing increasingly difficult for them to book larger and larger profits during the window between Horizon's shutdown and Kapiti's start of the day.

The losses continued to mount and Bullen knew he needed to do something, "I decided that first of all I had to sell some deep in-the-money options to stop the losses." He closed out several positions and reduced the desk's long exposure in the U.S. dollar down to approximately $211 million. It was a good move at the time and netted a profit of $13.4 million, but they were still carrying a huge loss, which meant further hiding.

The deception was weighing on Gianni Gray too. The young trader started worrying about the prospect of jail time should their scam be uncovered. In a phone conversation with Duffy, he voiced his fears, but his boss reassured him. "I would suggest a fucking custodial stay is fairly unlikely," Duffy told him. "You'll probably get a few thousand hours of fucking community service." Clearly, Duffy didn't think their actions were as criminal as they were. Or perhaps he was just trying to convince himself otherwise. After all, they'd gotten away with it for this long. All they needed was for the market to turn around, perhaps just a couple of good winning trades and they'd be back in business the way it was before.

A major obstacle appeared in the middle of October, when the bank's risk management system was upgraded. The old system was known to have flaws, to say the least, and one problem was the calculation of what are called the Greeks; the values assigned to the market sensitivities associated with the options market. In other words, calculating how sensitive an option is to movements in the underlying market, the time to maturity, etc.

The system also received an upgraded to their Value-at-Risk (VAR) calculations. VAR is essentially the amount of money a bank expects they can lose on a daily basis. Most banks use it in some form or another to measure their risk exposure. In the case of the National's FX options desk, the VAR limit was set at A$3.25 million per day. In other words, if there's a huge price swing in the market, the most the options book should expect to lose was A$3.25 million. Now, even though the traders were able to rig their profit reports, their position size didn't escape the upgraded system.

In fact, the new system showed that the desk's VAR was more than ten times their limit, pinning the number at A$40 million. Clearly, the new system was finally picking up their true risk-taking activities. Game over, right? Not quite so fast. In a last-ditch effort to save themselves, they argued that the numbers were nowhere near correct and the ridiculous new numbers did nothing but illustrate how the new-and-improved system was more flawed than the old one. In what can only be called a stroke of immensely good fortune, the bank's management actually believed them. The executives immediately lost faith in the upgraded system and ignored the VAR warnings.

That wasn't the only sign that was flashing red. During the month of October, the desk had 866 other individual breaches of their risk limits, all of which had been blindly approved by the Global Head of Foreign Exchange, Gary Dillon. But when Bullen was later confronted about it he only said, "We were over our limits and they were being signed-off on a daily basis. So my boss was aware."

The traders were having daily telephone conversations discussing their losses and the false trades, but they weren't the only ones. The business periodical *Derivatives Week* published an article about the NAB FX options desk, writing about the group's frantic selling of in-the-money options. The desk's positions had grown so large that they were now newsworthy, and apparently everyone in the market knew about them.

When October turned to November, there was an audible sigh of relief from our rogue traders. The market calmed down a little and options volatilities subsided. They were even able to book a legitimate A$4 million profit for the month. As per their standard, they booked some additional false profits, just for good measure, bringing their reported total profit to up to A$7.4 million. Buoyed with a little self-confidence in their still failed strategy, they increased their long position in the US dollar to $363 million.

The self-confidence they'd gained in November continued to grow into December, despite the new risk system showing off-the-chart numbers. When the new system produced a VAR risk number for the desk in excess of $300 million, the risk management group still assumed there was still a bug in the system. In their minds, there was no way any desk could have exceeded their limits by that much. And besides, the traders themselves had laughed it off as an obvious mistake. Bullen commented, "Looking over to the guys in market risk, we could sometimes see them laughing and mucking around. We would have tears in our eyes from considering that, twenty meters from them, the books were bubbling and threatening to blow up."

Given that there was no noticeable concern from anywhere else in the bank, the traders continued to increase their risk. They jacked up their long U.S. dollar position, bringing it up to a staggering $1.548 billion, which brought the desk's unhedged market exposure to more than $2 billion. Thanks to a brief rally in the U.S. dollar, they made back about A$16 million, but then the market reversed course and the value of the U.S. dollar continued to fall, ending the year down three cents against the Australian dollar. Their losses on December 31, 2003 had grown to A$91.8 million.

The walls were crumbling around them, and there was nothing they could do to stop the destruction. Spring would never arrive for the NAB 4.

*   *   *

In the early days of January 2004, they began discussing contingency plans. The reality of the situation had grown too large to ignore. They reasoned that the best option was for each of the traders to take a A$10 million loss annually for the next five years. They could theoretically cover their collective losses and have enough time to make back the money, assuming everything went according to plan. It was, essentially, a five-year plan to continuing hiding their losses.

That plan, however, went horribly awry. On Friday, January 2, an unexpected gain in the value of the Australian dollar sent their collective anxiety through the roof. Bullen recalled, "The Australian dollar kept rallying towards seventy-six cents, and over the following weekend I knew there would be major problems around the desk." Those "major problems" began to emerge on Monday, January 5, as Bullen sat at his desk. He knew they were finished. "I traced the shape of a mushroom cloud with my hands. It represented an atomic explosion."

That nuclear detonation summed up the group's position. They had blown themselves up. They were short between $1.2 and $1.4 billion Australian dollars, short $300-$500 million New Zealand dollars, long $100 million in U.S. dollars against the Japanese yen and short €40 million against the Australian dollar. As the value of the Australian dollar hit a high of .7660, things began to look even more bleak.

On Friday, January 9, an unknown member of the NAB 4 squad mentioned to a junior FX spot trader named Dennis Gentilin that he was concerned about the losses the FX options desk were carrying. The young Gentilin – who was visiting the Melbourne office from London – checked out their profit/loss reports. Finding no losses, he mentioned what he described as "suspicious transactions" to another trader, who in turn told Gary Dillon, the Global Head of FX trading, at 11 AM.

Caught seemingly unaware by this news, Dillon asked Gentilin to investigate it further. When he did, Gentilin noticed a A$40 million loss in the desk's spot FX positions. And while that loss was huge, it was still only the tip of the iceberg. Fortunately for the NAB 4, at least at the time, it was the only loss he uncovered. Gentilin then spoke with Bullen who would later describe it that he'd been "chatting with one of the spot guys who was down in Melbourne for

the week. He seemed genuinely interested in what we were doing."
Bullen was right. The "spot guy who was down in Melbourne" was,
in fact, really interested, just not in the way that Bullen thought.
Back at his desk, though, Bullen called another trader and informed
him that he'd seen Gary Dillon, who did not look terribly happy.
"The noose seemed to be tightening," Bullen later said.

Dillon spent the following weekend scouring over their positions. Despite his best efforts, all he was able to find was the A$40
million shortfall. It was enough of a loss to call the traders into the
office on Sunday to discuss it. The feeling amongst the NAB 4 was,
for the time being, still slightly optimistic. They were caught, but
not yet strung up to dry. "At this stage, though, there still seemed
to be a chance of getting out of it," Bullen recalled. He based this
optimism on the fact that Dillon had only managed to find the
A$40 million; he was still wasn't aware there was an additional
A$80 million loss still lurking.

The next Monday, the traders were operating under the belief
that they could continue adjusting their trades to hide their losses
from prying eyes, and minimize the losses that were already discovered. Their plan was to tell Dillon that they'd run the numbers
multiple times, and the resulting loss was a mere A$20 million, as
opposed to the A$40 million that he knew about. Once they got
past his wrath, they'd simply revert back to their old habits and
book a phantom A$20 million profit when the time was right.

They never got the chance. For Dillon, he had no choice but to
report the loss to his own boss, the General Manager of Markets
Ron Erdos. The end had begun for the NAB 4.

On Tuesday, January 13, the losses continued to grow. The bank
had no choice but to inform the Australian Prudential Regulation
Authority (APRA), the country's financial regulatory institution.
The NAB 4 traders began furiously deleting emails en masse at
6:30 the next morning, though the emails were later recovered by

forensic IT teams, the group managed to purge in excess of 14,000 electronic communications from their accounts.

That same afternoon, the National publicly announced a loss of A$180 million resulting from what they termed "irregular trades." When the news broke, Bullen said, "I knew my life as a currency options trader was probably coming to an end."

Throughout the remainder of the week, other traders were assigned the task of covering back various positions the group had, in the vain hope of recouping some of the money. It didn't work. By January 19, the losses had inched a little higher to A$185 million, but they would continue to grow before it was all over.

The traders were invited to continue coming to the bank's office, though they were reassigned to a conference room on the 36th floor. That would be their home for the next few days, as they met with representatives from various departments in the bank, as well as the bank's lawyers. They were told that if they continued cooperating, there was a chance the bank would not press charges, thus saving them from any kind of prison sentence. "I knew the bank had holes everywhere," Bullen said about the meetings, "and that the people inside the bank would be trying to cover their own backs. The head of market risk was in a minor panic, and I sensed fear."

In that spirit of cooperation, all the traders – except for Ficarra – submitted to taped interviews during which they were asked about their illicit activities. Ficarra, under advice from his lawyer, submitted a written statement about his involvement. For several days, the group pored over their positions with the various departmental representatives, who worked on checking losses and matching the one-sided internal trades that had been fictitiously booked. When all was said and done, it was discovered that some of their volatility estimates were also incorrect, which further increased the losses.

On January 27, 2004, NAB restated their original loss. That number grew to A$360 million, about $310 million in U.S. dollars.

In the end, the announcement caused a massive sell-off in NAB's stock, erasing A\$2 billion in market capitalization within the space of a few days. Due to the complexity and scope of the fraud, the questioning continued through February. The traders were suspended – with full pay – for a period of time, but were then finally terminated on March 12, 2004.

The axe that severed the NAB 4's ties to the bank didn't stop with the four traders, however. Chief Executive Officer Frank Cicutto – together with several members of the Board of Directors – resigned, and Cicutto was replaced with John Stewart, who commented, "We need more brave people that are prepared to confront bad behaviors." Gary Dillon was fired, as was Ron Erdos. The APRA swooped in and began their own investigation, generating a report that required significant changes at the bank, including raising substantial amounts of new capital to continue operating and the dissolution of its currency options business.

It would not be a happy ending for the NAB 4 traders. They would face trial in Australia, but that would take some time. When it finally began, Luke Duffy was the first to face the court, where he admitted at his appearance, "I have fucked up and I have led a few people down the wrong path with me." In a plea deal he struck with prosecutors, he pled guilty to three charges and received a 29 month prison sentence. In exchange, he testified against both Bullen and Ficarra, two of the people he, by his own admission, had led "down the wrong path."

Both Bullen and Ficarra pled not-guilty to all the charges they faced, despite the mountain of evidence – paired with Duffy's own testimony – that pointed to their guilt. Bullen opted to represent himself in court, ignoring the sage advice about a man who represents himself in court having a fool for a client. He was rewarded for his services with three years and eight months in prison. He grew a beard and dove more deeply into his study of Buddhism, saying, "The less money and fewer possessions I have, the less there will be to worry about."

Ficarra, under advice from his lawyer, attempted to use the same tactic employed by Nazi war criminals at Nuremburg. He was, he claimed, acting in good faith and doing nothing more than what he'd been told to do. "We started like an average person," he said, "and through ambition got, you know, jobs and a bit of power." In closing, he pleaded with the judge for leniency with a tactic didn't work: "Jail is not for me," he said. But just as the tribunal at Nuremburg disagreed with the Nazis, so, too, did the judge overseeing Ficarra's case. He was found guilty on twelve different charges and, despite his protestations to the contrary, it was determined that jail was, in fact, for him. Or at least it would be for two years and four months.

Gianni Gray, knowing that there was little-to-no hope to avoid prison time, fell on his sword and pled guilty to all charges. In sentencing him to a prison term of 16 months, the judge said, "I also accept that profit was perceived as being the be-all and end-all of the business, and that you somehow became swept up and carried along by the personality of Mr. Duffy."

While the scam concocted and perpetuated by the NAB 4 itself should be more than enough to make the average investor's blood boil, there is another fact that should further enrage that same average investor: the fact that the bank had no idea what was happening. PriceWaterhouseCoopers, in a report released following their own investigation, pointed out that the bank did nothing to solve the problem. "Our investigations indicate," they wrote, "that the culture fostered the environment that provided the opportunity for traders to incur losses, conceal them and escape detection, despite ample warning signs." In other words, there was clearly a business environment that fostered and encouraged illegal activities. The bank had not paid attention to what was happening inside their own building, and for that, they should be held accountable. Though the rogue traders were held accountable for their actions, not all of the criminals received punishment.

JP MORGAN AND THE LONDON WHALE, 2012

In 1851, Herman Melville published one of the classics of American literature, *Moby Dick*. It's a well-known story about Captain Ahab's hunt for the great white whale that took his leg, but it's actually based on the tragedy of the whaleship *Essex*, a Nantucket ship that, in November of 1820, was rammed by a sperm whale in the South Pacific. The crew of twenty sailors scrambled into three small whaleboats as the *Essex* sank. The final survivors were plucked from the sea on April 8, 1821 after spending nearly six months floating aimlessly. When the crew was reunited, only eight of the original twenty had survived the harrowing experience. The men who did survive had resorted to cannibalism, feeding on the bodies of their fellow sailors as they waited to be rescued.

Historians and others have speculated endlessly about the sinking of the *Essex*. Did the whale understand that it was a ship carrying people bent on killing it? Or did the whale simply view the ship's hull as a more generic threat? The answer will never be known for sure, but it remains a great story of the hunters becoming the hunted. George Pollard, the man who was the captain of the *Essex*, never spoke about his experience and eventually returned to sea again aboard another Nantucket whaleship, the *Two Brothers*, which also sank under his command. As Melville suggested in *Moby Dick*, perhaps there was a deeper force driving Pollard. Perhaps there was an element of revenge in his decision to return to whaling, a need to seek revenge on the beast that had almost killed him.

At its core, *Moby Dick* is a story of one man's single-minded obsession to kill the whale that took his leg. The reward for killing a whale *did* include the vast financial rewards that a ship's captain might reap, but there was also a component of self-glorification. It was an egotistical and vengeful quest that, in the end, lead to Ahab's own destruction. In *Moby Dick*, the captain is killed by his own tools; the line attached to the harpoon that he throws at Moby Dick loops around Ahab's neck, taking him under the water to his death. Ahab is destroyed by the instrument of his own vengeance.

In the arena of rogue traders, there's sometimes the same dichotomy driving their actions. They are, of course, driven by the desire to make money. But while the money is an attractive factor, there is another force at work too. Specifically, human vanity. Some traders who defy laws and regulations in their quest for "the big trade" can be as concerned with their own reputation as their financial status. In fact, you could argue that the two are linked: with more money comes greater status in the world of trading. Like Ahab, a trader's glory comes from pulling off the impossible; recognition results from being one of the best traders in the world.

Achieving the status of a top trader takes more than just luck. Not only do they have incredible intelligence and market understanding, but they're also willing to take enormous risk. George Soros broke the Bank of England in 1994 and became a famous billionaire as a result. John Paulson bet that the U.S. real estate market would crash in 2007; two years and $3 billion later, he was considered a financial genius. Paul Tudor Jones made $100 million for himself by shorting stocks in October 1987, just before the infamous Black

Monday stock market crash. But for every success story, there are countless traders on the other side with their stories now being told in *Rogue Traders*. Oftentimes the failures are the result of overexposure to risky financial instruments that turned against them, leaving them in an impossibly deep hole. And like Ahab, they are destroyed by the tools of their trade.

One would-be success story that was felled by an obsessive pursuit is that of Frenchman Bruno Michel Iksil, the man dubbed, ironically enough, the London Whale.

*   *   *

The harpoon that brought down the London Whale is called the credit default swap (CDS), an instrument that JP Morgan itself invented in 1994. CDS came into existence as a result of another maritime disaster, the Exxon Valdez oil spill off the coast of Alaska. The story goes that Exxon was a long-time client of JP Morgan and the oil company was expecting a huge regulatory fine in excess of $5 billion following the massive spill; they turned to JP Morgan for a credit line of $4.8 billion to cover it.

The request put the executives at JP Morgan in a moral bind. On the one hand, Exxon was a valuable client and had been for quite some time. Ordinarily, such a credit request would be extended without a second thought. However, the size of the spill was such that it presented a public relations nightmare for Exxon as much as a financial one, and, there was no way of knowing how the company would come out in the end. By extending a multi-billion-dollar credit line, JP Morgan would be exposing itself to risk in the event of Exxon's default. On the other hand, if JP Morgan declined granting the line of credit, it would have equally been a public relations fiasco because it would send the message that they had concerns about Exxon's ability to pay them back.

Blythe Masters, who today is one of the top-ranking women on Wall Street, led a team of JP Morgan analysts as they came up with the perfect solution to simultaneously allow the bank to extend credit to Exxon while minimizing their risk. The idea was quite simple, actually, and was based on the fact that the credit line was just like a bond sold to investors. Like any debt, it came with some risk of default; in this case, the risk was higher than the bank's executives were comfortable with. If the risk itself could be quantified, it could be sold off the same way as a bond.

And that's just what the folks at JP Morgan did. They sold the credit exposure to Exxon to another bank, the European Bank of Reconstruction and Development (EBRD). Exxon got their line of credit, JP Morgan provided the money, and EBRD took the default risk. JP Morgan kept one of their largest clients happy and did so without over-exposing themselves to tremendous risk. Meanwhile, in exchange for assuming the risk, EBRD was paid a handsome sum. In short, everybody was happy. And thus was born the credit default swap.

In 1997, JP Morgan expanded the model they created for Exxon by selling off a portion of their own loan portfolio's credit exposure to a group of investors. The end result was the same: the investors made some money and the bank reduced its risk. It was like the coming of age of mortgage-backed securities back in the 1980s all over again, both simple and ingenious. It just took a brilliant mind like Blythe Masters to see it for the first time.

It's easiest to think of a CDS as a form of insurance. For example, when you buy car insurance, you're protecting yourself in the event of an accident. The insurance company, on the other hand, is agreeing to cover the cost of an accident, if one occurs. At least that's how it's supposed to work. And if we've learned nothing else at this point, it's clear that things in the financial world oftentimes don't work exactly the way they're intended to.

In order to cover their risk, the insurance company charges an annual premium for the guarantee. Of course, they'll analyze your past driving record in order to determine the risk in the same way that a bank will analyze credit-worthiness before lending money. A CDS works much the same way, with one party getting relieved of an underlying debtor (like a corporation) defaulting on their loan payments (the financial equivalent of a car accident), and the other getting paid to take the risk. The seller of a CDS is like the insurance company; agreeing to compensate the buyer in the event of a default. They're basically assuming the credit risk from the buyer.

A CDS can be bought on just about anything with credit attached to it. That is, any entity out there, be it a country, a bank, or corporation; anything with a chance of default. And, it's not limited to a single issuer, there are CDS contracts written on baskets of bonds, indexes, and other combinations of corporate credits.

Again, like insurance, the chance of a credit event – like a default on a loan – is reflected in the price of the CDS; also called the spread. That's how much the buyer is willing to pay the seller for the coverage. The premium is paid on a quarterly basis and the payments are based on the face value of the contract. So a CDS contract of $1 million with a spread of 100 basis points will have an annual payment of 1.00% of the face value, or the buyer paying $10,000 annually to the seller.

The CDS spread is just like a credit score for a company. A higher spread indicates a greater fear that the borrower will default, and because of that fear, the seller charges a higher premium. If a buyer bought that same $1 million CDS contract based on a high-yield bond, the spread might be 150 basis points (indicating higher risk) and the annual fee for the insurance would rise to $15,000.

Conversely, if the contract was made on a top-rated company, the spread might only be 50 basis points.

The invention of the CDS allowed banks to protect themselves against defaults and drops in credit for the first time; allowing them to transfer credit risk from one party to another. Initially, banks were big winners from the development of the CDS because they could never before hedge their credit exposure. After the advent of the credit default swap, banks could retain the bonds or loans that they owned and transfer the credit risk to someone else. At first, it helped bankers sleep a little easier at night knowing that their multi-billion dollar portfolios could be insured against a financial crisis.

Of course, this wouldn't be much of a story if there wasn't another side, a darker side. And there is another side. As market participants caught wind of the new financial instrument and the potential for gains, a broader market developed. And, as this market grew, buyers were no longer just hedging their own underlying assets. Suddenly CDS became an instrument of outright speculation.

This was a major turning point in the history of the CDS market. The whole conservative part of hedging credit exposure began to disappear. When you buy life insurance, you can't buy it on someone else's life, nor can you buy homeowner's insurance on your neighbor's house. As the CDS market grew, you could effectively do just that. Investors bought insurance to cover a financial entity that they had no actual stake in. They bought CDS contracts if they thought a company might default; they sold them if they thought the company's credit would improve and CDS speculation became the favored way to trade the credit markets.

Growth in the market even led to the development of indexes that tracked an entire market segment, which became collectively known as the CDX Indexes. The indexes are the largest forum for investors seeking to bet on the likelihood of a group of company defaults. They made it even easier for investors to buy and sell protection as speculative bets. One company – Markit Group, Ltd. – owns and operates the indexes in the U.S. They created the North American CDX indexes in the U.S. – abbreviated as CDX.NA – and in Europe the equivalent index is the iTraxx.

Markit Group issues two new sets of credit indexes every year with a revised list of 125 companies contained in each new index. It's like the Dow Jones Industrial Average, except there's a new index created each year. The investment-grade (IG) index is composed of those companies deemed to be very credit-worthy and not likely to default. It's a way to speculate on a group of highly rated companies. The high-yield (HY) index, by contrast, is made up of companies with lower credit ratings and a higher risk of default. Each group has two-, five- and ten-year maturities, and each specific swap contract has a timeframe attached to it. For example, the 10-year North American High-Yield CDS index would be abbreviated as CDX.NA.HY.10Y.

The CDS market as a whole experienced exponential growth from the time of its launch. In 1998, the market was worth approximately $300 billion. Within four years, that number had ballooned to $2 trillion. In 2007, just before the financial crisis, the CDS market was valued at $62.2 trillion. Even today, as financiers still work to pick up the pieces after the destruction wrought by the financial crisis, the CDS market is worth an estimated $38.6 trillion. And, as the market expanded, it grew around by a collection of fourteen banks that serve as the main buyers and sellers; four banks in the United States account for 90% of all trades. And JP Morgan – the bank that started it all – is by far the largest market-maker of CDS in the world.

*　　*　　*

Legendary financier J.P. Morgan began his banking career in 1857, working for his father at the nascent Peabody, Morgan & Co. In 1871, he joined forces with the Drexel family, another financial stalwart, to create Drexel, Morgan & Company. Then, with the death of Anthony Drexel in 1893, Morgan took over as sole proprietor of the bank, renaming it J.P. Morgan & Company. By the beginning of the twentieth century, J.P. Morgan's bank was one of the world's most important financial institutions, having overseen such mergers as that of Edison General Electric and Thomson-Houston Electric Company to create General Electric, the creation of U.S. Steel, and American Telephone and Telegraph (AT&T).

Because of its size and status, J.P. Morgan & Company was forced to assume the role of central bank of the United States following the financial panic of 1907, when the New York Stock Exchange lost nearly half its value and bank runs spread like wildfires. J.P. Morgan publicly called for banks across the country to inject capital into the financial system, pledging much of his own personal wealth to help save the country's economy. The gambit worked and the ensuing Congressional investigation into the panic eventually led to the creation of the Federal Reserve six years later.

A century later, world markets faced another massive crisis as the real estate market imploded and stocks plummeted. Investment banks that had weathered storms of the past like Bear Stearns and Lehman Brothers collapsed, their corpses lying as stark reminders of the fragility the world's financial system. But JP Morgan, under the guidance of CEO Jamie Dimon, not only survived the catastrophe, but emerged stronger than its competitors. Dimon attained rock-star status among bank CEOs for his skillful navigation of the financial crisis and his superb risk-management. Dimon declared

JP Morgan to have a "fortress balance sheet," and the CEO himself is described as "a risk-averse manager who demands regular and exhaustive reviews of every corner of the bank."

Today, JP Morgan is the largest bank in the United States, with over $2.4 trillion in assets and 240,000 employees spread across 5,500 bank branches and corporate offices. They are also the single largest derivatives dealer in the world, including their perch atop the lucrative CDS market.

One of the qualities that had helped JP Morgan survive the crisis of 2008 was the bank's massive cash reserves. In 2005, the bank was flush with cash and the executives felt they needed a dedicated investment office to handle those reserves, an amount that grew even larger after the 2008 panic when investors saw JP Morgan as the safest bank to keep their cash. The Chief Investment Office (CIO) was created to oversee those funds, and by 2012, it was managing a $350 billion portfolio of excess reserves, as well as two smaller portfolios of JP Morgan pension funds.

The group was headed by woman named Ina Drew. A graduate of Johns Hopkins University, Drew was 55 years old and one of the highest-ranking women on Wall Street, having previously served as the global treasurer of JP Morgan. She was also, perhaps not surprisingly, one of the highest-paid executives at JP Morgan with a 2010 compensation package that topped out at $15 million. She was neither apologetic nor modest, as she boasted to shareholders that she was "instrumental in setting the course and directing the firm's repositioning of the balance sheet." Part of that repositioning effort included pushing the bank to expand the investments of the CIO portfolio and adding a trading outpost in the bank's London office.

The man who was put in charge of that outpost was Achilles Macris, a Greek national and U.S. citizen. An aggressive trader – commonly referred to as a "big hitter" by many colleagues – Macris was known for unconventional thinking when it came to trading, a strategy that served him well. He was well-educated and demonstrated extensive knowledge of art, wine, politics and history, and was known to be quite blunt with other employees. Perhaps not out of character, he owned a six-foot-by-six-foot painting of a missile in flight that hung on the wall of his London apartment. By 2012, the CIO staff consisted of 400 employees split between New York and London, with New York serving as command central and Macris running the London office.

The CIO's mandate from the executive suites in Manhattan was to "optimize and protect [the organization's] balance sheet from potential losses." In other words, the group was charged with hedging the bank's assets as a whole, though outsiders argued that their sole purpose was to insulate JP Morgan from another financial crisis. Regardless of the true purpose, the CIO office was never intended to function as a proprietary trading desk whose sole purpose was to make money. The portfolio was supposed to be used to "generate earnings for [the bank], and also [to balance out] interest-rate risk," according to one JP Morgan executive. The CIO traders were supposed to invest in relatively safe investments – plain vanilla products like U.S. Treasury bonds, municipal bonds, corporate bonds and high-grade mortgage-backed securities. It was, at its core, the manifestation of a typical Jamie Dimon mantra: minimize the bank's risk through safe investments. But with the infusion of cash following the 2008 crisis, the CIO portfolio doubled in size and the traders needed to find new investments for their funds.

Those new products were placed under the rubric of the Synthetic Credit Portfolio, the creation of Achilles Macris. This new portfolio was the CIO's expansion into derivatives on corporate and mortgage debt, a clear deviation from the original philosophy of hedging. It was the beginning of a shift away from hedging JP Morgan's risk exposure into speculative trading, a shift that highlighted the blurred line between proprietary trading and hedging on Wall Street.

During the financial crisis, the CIO team used their cash to purchase more speculative investments. While other banks were dumping securities at fire-sale prices, the JP Morgan CIO traders were snapped them up. They amassed a huge position in collateralized debt obligations (CDOs), as well as CDS in high-yield indexes, both were within the scope of the low risk-tolerance models established by the bank. The traders bought AAA-rated CDOs, and CDS that were positioned to pay in the event that a company with a low credit rating defaulted. Given the economic climate at the time, AAA-rated bonds were the only CDOs worth holding, and the likelihood of a company with credit defaulting seemed pretty good. The Synthetic Credit Portfolio took in approximately $4 billion in distressed assets by December 2008 and generated about $170 million in profits for the year. It was, by just about anyone's standards, a phenomenal result given the year's turmoil in the financial markets.

The following year was even better for the CIO desk. They made significant purchases of distressed European government securities, as well as mortgage- and asset-backed securities. And, of course, they bought plenty of CDS. On June 1, 2009, when General Motors filed for bankruptcy, in a move that lead to a massive government bail-out, the traders at JP Morgan rejoiced because the CDS positions they were holding were suddenly incredibly valuable. That year, the CDS positions alone generated $1.05 billion in profits. The CIO desk was suddenly thrust into the spotlight and its traders regaled as heroes at the firm. The SCP book became one of the best trading books at the entire bank, if not the single best. But they still felt they could make even more money, if only they weren't constrained by their risk limits.

Among the traders was a Spaniard named Javier Martin-Artajo. He had been hired by Macris in 2007 and quickly rose to become the Head of Credit Equity Trading. He was a tall man with a rugged attractiveness that reminded many of actor Jon Hamm, famous for his role as Don Draper in the television series *Mad Men*. From Macris' perspective, Marin-Artajo was a known quantity in the trading world. The Spaniard had worked previously for Macris at Dresdner Bank, where Martin-Artajo had served in the same capacity, overseeing that bank's credit-derivatives trading.

There was also a junior trader named Julien Grout, who joined the London office in 2009. Grout's main job was to value the positions and monitor their gains and losses. He was new to JP Morgan – and new to the profession, for that matter – so he was keen to do what he was told. He looked up to the more senior traders, clearly hoping to one day to become one of them, but for now, he was relegated to the position of student, learning from some of the best in the business.

And finally, there was Bruno Michel Iksil, a thirty-something Frenchman who was well-known in London's trading circles. He typically dressed in black jeans and open-necked shirts and was described as "not the sort of trader who drives a Ferrari and wears a Rolex." He was passionately prideful of his French heritage, though he was also known to be quiet and gentle in his demeanor. A 1991 graduate of the prestigious Grand École Centrale de Paris, Iksil was a skilled mathematician who was fond of starting discussions with mathematical jargon as a way of confusing the person with whom he was talking. It was also a defense mechanism, whenever he was challenged about something, it was a way of showing his self-confidence and intellectual superiority. He lived just outside of Paris, commuting every Monday to London and returning to his home country on Friday night. Colleagues referred to him as a "monster trader," though at JP Morgan, Iksil was the senior CIO trader in London. In time, he would earn the nickname The London Whale.

*   *   *

By 2010, the CIO began pushing to change their risk model, hoping to install a one to more accurately reflect their true risk-taking. Of course, the new model they proposed would also lower their risk profile, making it look like they were taking less risk. For the desk, a change in the model was more than just a pat on the back from their superiors for achieving great results, it would be a green light to take more risk and achieve even better results. If they did it right – and judging by the last two years, they knew how to – it would translate into a lot more money come bonus time.

Initially, the CIO's risk model was based on the 1988 Basel Accord, or Basel I. It was the first set of rules established by the Basel Committee on Banking Supervision in Basel, Switzerland. The rules established a minimum capital threshold for banks, based on formulas to risk-weight assets. This first collection of regulations – there were two subsequent updates – was primarily concerned with credit risk. The assets held by a bank were divided into different categories: cash, for example, was weighted at 0% risk, whereas AAA-rated mortgage-backed securities were weighted at 20%. The higher the risk associated with the security, the higher the percentage assigned to it. Under Basel I, banks like JP Morgan were required to hold capital equal to at least 8% of their risk-weighted assets.

One of the major criticisms of Basel I was that it did a poor job of estimating risk correlation. Basel I assumed that if there was a single corporate default, it would lead to more defaults. In other words, the model assumed an inevitable domino effect and, as a result, produced risk weightings that were relatively high. The CIO traders and even JP Morgan's own risk management team were among those who believed the Basel I was too conservative and generated higher VaR[7] (Value at Risk) numbers than were warranted.

Achilles Macris was the driving force behind the amazing gains the desk realized in 2008 and 2009. The old guard at JP Morgan might have seen him as too much of a risk-taker, but they couldn't argue with the results. Surprisingly, the next year, the bank's management decided to cut the size of their CDS positions; revenues, in turn, took a steep dive as a result, with the Synthetic Credit Portfolio only booking a profit of $149 million for the year. While still a healthy amount of money, it was nowhere near the billion-plus level they booked just a year earlier. It was clear to anyone who was paying attention that the SCP could make significant amounts of money, if they were just unshackled from their Basel I risk limits.

During the middle of 2011, Iksil was back in the market in a big way. His analysis suggested that the credit markets in Europe were on the verge of deteriorating rapidly. There was financial uncertainty from the European sovereign debt crisis which was gripping the continent. Iksil believed that the turmoil roiling through the sovereign markets in Ireland, Spain, Portugal, and Greece would spread to the corporate credit markets, so he began buying a large position in high-yield CDS indexes that were set to mature at the end of 2011, while selling protection in the investment-grade CDS index at the same time. He was betting that companies with weak

---

[7] Value at Risk (VaR) is a common way for banks and financial institutions to measure the risk associated with an investment, and most banks use one form of a VaR model to measure their risk. VaR is supposed to estimate the maximum amount that a particular investment – a portfolio, a specific trading position, or an individual security – can lose during the course of a single day, with that number pegged to a statistical confidence level. For example, a portfolio of securities might be determined, based on average market moves, to possibly lose at most $1 million 95% of the time. In that example, the value at risk would be $1 million. When the CIO portfolio began trading, the desk was assigned a VaR of $5 million, meaning they could hold positions that were not supposed to lose more than $5 million on any given day.

credit ratings – the high-yield credits – would suffer, whereas high-grade companies would survive relatively unscathed.

Basically, Iksil was counting on a credit event – some sort of corporate default – in the high-yield index before December 31, 2011. He ran the position up to a long of $217 billion in the high-yield index and short $166 billion in the investment-grade index. The net position boiled down to a long of $51 billion in credit default swaps which was a huge bet for a high-yield company default. In other words, if there was a significant high-yield credit default, Iksil would look like a genius.

A group of hedge funds figured they'd found a sucker in Iksil, and decided to bet against him. Basically, they were convinced that there would be no defaults in high-yield companies before the end of the year. Perhaps they thought the financial storm wasn't quite as strong as it seemed, or perhaps they thought they had some extrasensory knowledge about the market. Whatever their reason, they took the opposite bet. The line in the sand was drawn and someone was going to make a lot. On the other side of that line, someone was going to lose a lot.

By the middle of November, it looked like Iksil had bet wrong. You could imagine the hedge fund traders thinking about how to spend the bonuses after schooling the Frenchman on the finer points of CDS trading. But then, on November 29 – just one month before the CDS contracts were set to expire – AMR Corp, the parent company of American Airlines, filed for bankruptcy. The credit event triggered a massive payoff in the high-yield index, making Iksil over $550 million in a single day. That mammoth windfall offset the $100 million in losses that the desk was carrying for the year, bringing their profit for 2011 up to $453 million.

Iksil had finally made a name for himself. JP Morgan executives were suddenly full of confidence with their trading wunderkind who had managed to foresee AMR Corp's impending bankruptcy. Ina

Drew wrote to Jamie Dimon that "the fourth quarter 400 million gain was the result of the unexpected American Airlines default." The key word is "unexpected." Whether Iksil had an inkling that it was going to happen or whether he'd just gotten lucky didn't matter so much. What *did* matter was that he'd gone toe-to-toe with the hedge funds and came out on top. One of those hedge fund traders would later say, "It seemed like the trade of the century to be long the index."

Outside of the confines of JP Morgan, however, Iksil was not the same celebrated rock star trader that he was inside. The hedge funds who had picked the wrong side of the bet were bitter and felt that Iksil had nothing more than absurdly good luck. Within a month of losing his shirt, a major corporation suddenly declared bankruptcy in a move that few financial prognosticators had even remotely suspected. To them, Iksil was just lucky. And stubborn. His refusal to back down from the trade – despite the fact that he'd won in the end – earned him the nickname "The Caveman" throughout the market. It was the first of three nicknames that would trail him during his professional life.

Iksil didn't let the names and the insults affect him though. He was at the top of the mountain, the man who had just made a killing. He had wielded massive trading positions and realized a huge profit, all the while riding the high that comes with exorbitant risk-taking. His reputation was growing by leaps and bounds and he finally qualified as a top trader in the financial circles. The seeds of an Ahab-like obsession had been sewn and they were beginning to take root.

*   *   *

One month after Iksil's "trade of the century" had rolled off and 2012 began, he was left short his investment-grade index totaling approximately $51 billion. In every way, Iksil's prospects for the coming year looked promising. Unfortunately, those prospects turned rather quickly. The year began with a bankruptcy just when he was short the market. On January 19, Eastman Kodak filed for bankruptcy and those who were long the indexes received a hefty payday, and, unfortunately for Iksil, he wasn't one of them. Fortunately for him, though, Kodak was part of the high-yield group and it didn't affect Iksil's investment-grade index directly. It meant Iksil missed out on the opportunity to start 2012 with another massive gain, but it was worse than just a missed opportunity. As a result of the Kodak bankruptcy, all of the CDS indexes rallied and Iksil's short position in investment-grade CDS was one of them. The day of the bankruptcy, his book lost about $22 million; within a week, that loss had grown to $67 million, and by the first day of February, the book would be down a total of $100 million.

At the same time in January, the corner office dwellers at JP Morgan were so happy with Iksil's trading in 2011 that they rewarded him with an even larger trading budget for 2012. Ina Drew wanted Iksil to recreate the American Airlines situation that had made him a half-a-billion dollars. She was probably unaware that they just missed that opportunity when Kodak went bust on January 19th. The good news didn't stop there, however. In addition to the budget increase, management wanted the CIO team to reduce the amount of regulatory capital that they were using. Essentially, it meant lowering their risk-weighted assets (RWA) as calculated by the Basel I risk weightings. In a move that wasn't unique on Wall Street, management wanted them to decrease the size of their positions yet still make more money. Specifically, the executives wanted them to reduce their RWA by $25 billion, just when Iksil was swimming in a loss.

When Ina Drew asked Iksil about the cost of reducing their RWA by less than half that amount – a trifle $10 billion – Iksil responded that it would cost approximately $516 million because they'd have to sell their CDS positions. In response, Drew replied, "Let's review the unwind plan to maximize [profit/loss]. We might have a tad more room on RWA." Whether or not that review ever took place is immaterial; there were no more discussions about reducing the size of the SCP holdings. Clearly nobody in the CIO group wanted to start the year by taking a massive loss.

Given that the easiest way to reduce their RWA was to offload positions – and that was tossed out as not being practical – the traders needed another a way to achieve what seemed to be an impossible goal. But as it often seems, the solution was so simple that it was hiding in plain sight. The easiest way was to simply change their risk calculation model. The old Basel I model was outdated and everyone agreed. Fortunately for the traders, there had been a series of updates to the original Basel Accord, and the latest and greatest of those updates was Basel III. They decided to request that their risk model be updated to be compliant with that new set of rules.

If there is one thing a Wall Street analyst loves, it's a loophole. And that's just what the Basel III accord provided them. By using the new Basel III model, the CIO's VaR would be immediately cut in half. They hastily sent a request for the new VaR model to the appropriate people to review. Just by changing the methodology for calculating risk, they would be able to almost double the amount of risk they could take and still be compliant with the firm's guidelines. They could meet their goal of cutting their RWA by $25 billion without having to cut the size of their positions and incur the loss. Clearly a win–win situation. They crossed their fingers and knew that if it passed, they would have new trading opportunities.

On January 30, 2012, the Model Review Group authorized the CIO Market Risk Group to begin using the new risk model, and both Jamie Dimon and Ina Drew signed off on the approval. The CIO desk managed to accomplish what was seemed the impossible. Within weeks of their official request, they were simultaneously reducing their risk exposure and maintaining their position size. On top of that, they had just empowered themselves to take even more risk. It was a dream come true for Iksil and the other traders. The shackles holding them back had been removed and now they were free to ramp up their positions.

*   *   *

Despite the fact that that one problem had been solved, Iksil was still in a bind. They were carrying a large loss. But their risk limits had just been lifted, which meant that there was a way out. There is almost nothing that traders like more than a winning trade, and Iksil knew exactly what to do. He'd go long the high-yield credit index and short the investment-grade index. It had worked many times before, so why not one more time? Macris liked the move and gave Iksil the go-ahead to begin buying the high-yield indexes and selling the investment-grade indexes. It was almost an exact replica of what they'd done in 2011. It seemed too easy.

And, truth be told, it was too easy. First, the indexes were already trading at relatively high prices due to the bankruptcies of both AMR Corp and Eastman Kodak. So while Iksil was buying, he was doing so at inflated prices. Then, in an attempt to generate more income to offset the losses, he was selling much more of the investment-grade index to pay for owning the high-yield index.

Fundamentally, the strategy made sense. High-yield corporate credits are, statistically, more likely to default and Iksil was banking on that fact. But it was a little more than that. Iksil and company saw very little chance for an investment-grade default, so that large short position just didn't seem very risky. But there are more ways to lose money on an investment than a default. For starters, the price can go against you. Clearly, Iksil was risking everything that the index he was short-selling would not move against him. That index would become famous in the world of CDS – it's called the CDX.NA.IG9.10Y. In layman's terms, it's the North America Investment-grade Index Series 9, created in 2007 with an underlying set of 125 corporate bonds with investment-grade ratings. By 2012, the number of companies remaining had dropped to 121, and those companies were still financially strong. They included names like Wal Mart and MBIA Insurance. From Iksil's vantage point, they seemed like a pretty safe bet.

On January 25th, Iksil sold $2.78 billion worth of protection in the CDX.NA.IG9.10Y at an average spread of 126.5 basis points. With such a large seller, the index began to decline immediately, which was good for Iksil. Buoyed by that initial success, he sold an additional $2.17 billion on the following day, this time at an average spread of 120.64 basis points. By the end of the trading day, the market closed at a price of 117.5 basis points, booking a nice mark-to-market profit at the end of January which allowed them to get back some of the money they'd lost earlier in the month. Iksil was convinced the market would continue to move in his favor, especially with his help moving it that way.

This time around, however, it wouldn't be so simple. The hedge funds that Iksil had beaten down at the end of 2011 were back. Not only were they still smarting from the blows they'd taken, but they were lined up against him again, intent on extracting revenge. The ring-leader was a hedge fund called Saba Capital Management, founded by Boaz Weinstein. Weinstein was an accomplished chess master, as well as an expert blackjack and poker player. He'd started his career at Deutsche Bank, where he specialized in CDS trading. For ten years, he was one of that firm's shining stars, culminating in a $1.5 billion profit in 2007. His luck then turned in 2008, when he posted a staggering $1.8 billion loss. This would be his swan song at Deutsche Bank, and he founded his hedge fund the following year.

Saba Capital Management – named after the Hebrew word for "grandfatherly wisdom" – started in August of 2009 with $140 million in capital with the support of Weinstein's former employer, Deutsche Bank. He took fifteen traders with him to build up his strategy in the credit default swaps market, and, by 2012, Saba's assets had mushroomed to $5.8 billion.

Saba and several other hedge funds knew that the CDS indexes were being pushed around by Iksil's oversized bets, and despite their losing bet against him, they knew there would be an opportunity arising from the JP Morgan trader's huge positions. In fact, by the end of January, Iksil's positions were the largest the CDS market had ever encountered. There were usually large price swings every time Iksil was in the market. Because of his ominous presence, the London banks began to refer to Iksil as "Voldemort," the villain in the Harry Potter books - the man who was so powerful that he couldn't be called by name. Iksil's nickname had now shifted from "Caveman" to "Voldemort," and it clearly indicated that he was growing increasingly sinister. He was now seen as an evildoer that needed to be destroyed, at least in the eyes of the CDS market.

On January 30, the index began moving higher, to a spread of 121 basis points. Iksil was still in-the-money on his recent sales, but the positions he had been holding since the beginning of the year were losing again. At this point, Iksil began losing faith in the trade and wanted to end it immediately. It was essentially an act of ripping off the Band-Aid in one quick motion. Take the losses and move on. He told Martin-Artajo that they should "take the pain fast" and get out of it. Sell it at a loss immediately before it got worse. It was only January, after all, they still had the whole year to recover.

It was a momentary burst of rational thinking from the otherwise glory-obsessed trader. But the moment quickly passed as Martin-Artajo simply told Iksil to "stop taking losses." It was typical of Martin-Artajo to give blank, generic instructions to his traders. He would tell them "don't lose money," but never give clear instructions on what he specifically wanted them to do. Of course, Iksil's job was to make money and Martin-Artajo was really just asking him to do his job.

The next day, on January 31st, the market moved against them again. At one point during the day, Iksil jumped out of his chair and shouted, "They're all against us!" It was, on the surface reminiscent of a boy crying foul because somebody was cheating in a game. But in the adult world of CDS trading, someone taking the opposite side of your trade doesn't qualify as cheating. The market was looking to square up for last year, and maybe even make a little extra money off Iksil to boot. Iksil ended the month by reporting that he had "tried to fight it in the last sessions and was unsuccessful," saying that the trading desk was "in full fight" against the market. Their best efforts, however, weren't nearly enough.

When the end of January reports were tallied, Iksil had run up a short position in the IG9 10Y to the tune of $278 billion against long positions in the HY10 and HY11 of $90 billion. The net result was a short almost $200 billion more in investment-grade credit index than the long in high-yield index. In other words, at this point, Iksil was doing the exact the opposite of the CIO's mandate of hedging the bank's risk. He was *adding* to their risk. The original hedging strategy had morphed into outright speculation. At the end of the day, the final tally for January showed a $100 million loss in the Synthetic Credit Portfolio.

In some trader's minds, losses don't really exist until the position is closed. That thinking has cost more than one trader his job. The reality is that something is worth only what someone else is willing to pay for it. If you don't like the price now, it doesn't mean it's still worth the same as it was last week. Traders who wait for the market to come back are often not facing reality and digging themselves into a deeper hole. And that reality, for Iksil, was about to become a very deep hole.

*   *   *

Given that Iksil's position were large enough to disrupt market prices, it should have sent out warning signals at JP Morgan corporate. In fact, risk alarms were going off and limits were being breached regularly, but those alarms were either ignored altogether or approved automatically. Iksil's trades would involve 330 individual risk limit violations just in the month of February. In the worst case scenario, the traders disputed the breaches and assured anyone who asked that everything was fine.

The hole was about to get even deeper. On February 2, 2012, Boaz Weinstein of Saba Capital Management was a speaker at the Harbor Investment Conference. Given his status as a major player in the CDS market, his presentation was taken as gospel by many those who heard it. During his speech, he publicly recommended buying the CDX.NA.IG9.10Y index, explaining that it had diverged from its fair value. Basically, he advocated that investors take the exact opposite position of Iksil. There was speculation out there that Weinstein was already long the index and was losing money, and, fearing a repeat of the previous November, he wanted to get more buyers on his side. In reality, he needed all the help he could get to move the market against JP Morgan and Iksil.

Regardless of his motivation, Weinstein got the message out to willing listeners, many of them hedge fund traders. Sentiment around the market grew that Iksil was overconfident and was hearkening back to his "Caveman" days. They agreed that Iksil couldn't keep perpetually selling the index so, when it came time to buy it back, they'd make a killing. It was just a matter of time and patience. They began buying the IG index. And then they waited.

Back at JP Morgan, the CIO traders were growing increasingly concerned about their mounting losses, but there was nothing they could do about it. They were committed to the trade, whichever way the wind blew. Getting out was not an option, but adding to the position was. Martin-Artajo, fearful of what might happen if the market continued to move higher, ordered the traders to "defend the positions."

"Defending a position" has sunk many traders many times before. As a trade moves against someone, sometimes human nature says to add to a losing position. The rational goes, "If I liked selling it at 113 basis points, I should love selling it at 120 basis points." When the market finally turns around, it doesn't have to move as much to make back the initial loss. And that was the strategy that Martin-Artajo's crew embraced. Over the course of the month of February, the CIO traders added another $75 billion in new positions.

2012 was a leap year, which meant there was one extra day in the month of February. At JP Morgan, that extra day was a day they'd come regret. On that 29th day, the CIO traders went on a selling spree. Within a three-hour period, they had sold another $4.6 billion of the CDX.NA.IG9.10Y index, which was more than half of the $7.17 billion they sold the entire day. They were hitting bids over and over again for a full three hours. On top of that, their trades accounted for 90% of the day's trading in the entire CDS index market. They knew that constant selling was the only way to keep it from moving against them. Anytime they were not selling, the index would begin to drift higher, just to be hammered back down when Iksil started selling again. By the end of the day, their efforts resulted in a $69 million loss for the month; you can imagine the size of the loss if Iksil hadn't been there to sell.

In the traders' defense, they were given contradictory orders. On the one hand, they were asked to reduce their risk and to make more money; on the other, they were told to "defend their positions" and not to lose money. They were effectively stuck in a no-win situation. But the losses were still growing and it presented a problem, especially for a group that was supposedly hedging the bank's risk. They needed to get creative with the math for the end-of-day reports on February 29th. They mismarked the IG9 10Y contract down to a spread of 115 basis points, when the actual end-of-day spread should have been 119 basis points. Just by changing the 9 to a 4 – theoretically a mistake anyone could have made after a long and stressful day – it hid much of their losses. Remember, one basis point on positions this size is a lot of money. The entire SCP trading book - longs and shorts together - lost $46 million for every uptick in prices. Mismarking that one contract by four basis points saved them approximately $132 million for month-end. It was a move that would later come back to haunt them.

The month of March would not be any better for the CIO team as the SCP portfolio continued its downward spiral. The group continued to lose money. The portfolio was being overwhelmed by the hedge fund consortium that was set up as a counter attack on the other side of their trade. Macris knew there was an impending doom hanging over them like a huge thunderhead and told his superiors, "We will not be able to defend our positions." Meetings were taking place round-the-clock, and the CIO traders were wracking their brains to come up with a solution. The only common thread in these discussions was the constantly dwindling value of the portfolio.

They were stuck in a horrible trade that offered no escape without huge financial consequences. However, they had been in a similar situation before just two months earlier and came up with a creative solution. That solution had been to change the way the calculated risk, thereby maintaining their holdings while showing a lower level of risk-taking. It had worked the first time, so logic dictated it might just work a second time. All they needed to do was to change the mark-to-market system to something that was slightly more favorable. And that's exactly what they did.

One of the reasons for marking-to-market a security or portfolio of securities is to see its value at a particular point in time. It's especially valuable in terms of comparing its value to another point in time. It also allows for a little fluidity in the pricing of securities and determining a portfolio's value. It's supposed to be the price at the end of the day. Period. The numbers won't lie. Except when they do.

Julien Grout, the junior trader, was in charge of reporting the prices at the end of the day, and he was using what is called the "crude mid." He took the bid and offer prices at the end of the day, and then took the mid-point between the two numbers. That number was the price they reported at the end of the day. It wasn't an exact science, to say the least, but it was the procedure they used for valuing their positions.

"Crude mid" is allowed under the Generally Accepted Accounting Principles (GAAP), so there were no conflicts of accounting integrity there. Things got a little more shady, however, when it was revealed that Grout wasn't always using the bid/spread prices at the end of the day. Martin-Artajo instructed Grout to stop using the end-of-day methodology and, unless there was a major event that moved the market, Grout was specifically instructed to find the most favorable bid/offer spread at any point during the day. In addition, he could take prices from any bank that would show him bids and offers, then use the best one for pricing positions. It was a pretty clear mandate: find the most favorable "crude mid" during the day and use it.

By the second week of March, Iksil knew the group had crossed the line between bending the rules and out-right breaking them; he became increasingly uncomfortable. Grout confirmed to Iksil that he was "not marking mids as per a previous conversation," and he also said that their new pricing method was nowhere near appropriate. Iksil then instructed Grout to keep a separate spreadsheet. Though they continued to enter the most favorable mid prices into the JP Morgan accounting system, they would keep a separate spreadsheet to record the real market values.

But by March 15, just a few days later, Iksil was still worried that their valuations were just not "realistic," to which Grout replied, "I'm trying to keep a relatively realistic picture here – ig9 10y aside." Iksil's frustration was obvious: "I don't know where [Martin-Artajo] wants to stop, but it's getting idiotic."

That same day, Iksil reported a loss in the trading book, despite Martin-Artajo's instruction "not to lose money." But again, there were two camps. Iksil wanted to realize the losses and get out, whereas Martin-Artajo just wanted to ignore the losses. The loss that Iksil recorded was merely $40 million, which quickly caught the attention of Martin-Artajo. He asked Iksil, "Why did you do that?" Iksil explained that the difference between their actual losses and the ones they had reported was up to $292 million. All he got in reply was, "What I don't understand at all is why you are explaining the, this way on the email?"

The next Monday, March 17, Iksil gave Grout specific instructions "to not make the additional effort to disguise the loss." He went on to describe their instructions from Martin-Artajo as "idiotic." Their losses continued to grow, and he estimated that the SCP book was really down about $600 million. Still, the total amount that was being reported to the firm – using the best mid-point price – was half of that, at only $300 million.

The rest of the week was not good for the CIO traders. Iksil knew that his future was in jeopardy: "I am going to be hauled over the coals...You don't lose 500 million without consequences." Those consequences soon began to take shape, when Ina Drew ordered the CIO traders to "put the phones down" and stop trading. The traders were informed that "Ms. Drew does not want any trades executed until we discuss it." For Iksil, he knew what was coming next. "It is over," he wrote in an email. "It is hopeless now. I tell you they are going to destroy us."

His words would become alarmingly prophetic, though he realized the gravity of the situation too late. When the desk stopped "defending the position," the market started to rise, further compounding their losses. On the last day of March, 2012, the investment-grade index had moved a full 38 full basis points against them since the beginning of the year. By "defending the position" to keep up the selling pressure, the short side of the portfolio had swelled to $157 billion. Achilles Macris sent JP Morgan's Chief Risk Officer and email saying that he had "lost confidence" in his team and he was requesting "help with the synthetic credit book."

The real mark-to-market for the last day of March should have shown a loss of $583 million. Iksil instructed Grout to tell Martin-Artajo that "it's more than 500, so he gets it." Martin-Artajo was unrelenting and told them that he wanted the loss adjusted down by at least $200 million. At 8:15 PM London time, Martin-Artajo told the New York office that they expected to close the books with a $150 million loss. Meanwhile, Iksil was working with Grout to help soften the financial blow, telling him, "We should probably do something cleaner, with a, you see, a lesser result." He suggested they book a loss of $250 million, which would come close to Martin-Artajo's request for a $200 million charge. At the same time, Iksil was unaware of the phone call to the New York office promising the $150 million loss. After Iksil left for the day, Grout scoured the prices for the day and adjusted the mark-to-market down even further, reporting a $138 million loss for the quarter at 8:41 PM. Martin-Artajo commended the junior trader for his "excellent" work.

Of course, that "excellent" work was grossly understating their loss. When asked by a risk officer how the portfolio's value was determined,

Martin-Artajo pleaded ignorance: "Hey, I ain't no accountant," he said. JP Morgan released their earnings report for the first quarter on April 13, 2012. Because the SCP portfolio was mismarked, JP Morgan had publicly understated the losses they'd sustained, and in so doing, they'd also broken a host of securities laws.

*　*　*

The first inkling that there was a problem at JP Morgan began to trickle out via the financial news on Sunday, April 6. A trader who was called "The London Whale" was reported to be holding an unimaginably large position in the credit default swaps, positions that were creating "unusually large price swings" whenever he was in the market. Reports that various hedge funds were lined up against him also circulated. Jamie Dimon didn't take the stories lightly and asked Ina Drew for a "full diagnostic" the following Monday.

After Dimon spent a week digesting Drew's report and consulted with other members of his management team, he announced on an earnings call that the whole affair was "a complete tempest in a teapot." In short, there was no story, because the losses they reported were accurate. In support of his boss, Chief Financial Officer Douglas Braunstein announced, "We are very comfortable with our positions." Clearly, they hoped that the story would fizzle out with their announcements. Their hopes were dashed, however, because the London Whale story continued to gain traction.

On April 27, JP Morgan's senior management, who were collectively growing tired of the accusations that they were hiding losses, asked a senior trader in their investment bank to value the CIO's positions. The results were staggering. The trader found that the quarter-end marks were at least $275 million higher than the real numbers, and the loss was at least $767 million greater than Iksil's spreadsheet. To say this was just a problem was equivalent to calling Mount Everest a gentle hill.

When the truth came to light, JP Morgan's management immediately removed the mark-to-market pricing responsibilities from the CIO office and assigned the entire SCP portfolio to the trader in the investment bank. Then, an unnamed JP Morgan executive issued a directive to all staff members not "to discuss [their work] with people outside the immediate group." The firm was in heavy damage-control mode, and that information was very valuable. The less that got out, the more that JP Morgan stood to gain. Or at least, the better the chances they could survive this storm.

On May 10, JP Morgan was forced to revise their earlier earnings report. This time, they reported a $2 billion loss on the SCP portfolio, attributed to the now-notorious London Whale. Dimon, in a rare example of self-effacement, said, "There were many errors, sloppiness, and bad judgment. These were egregious mistakes. They were self-inflicted." Dimon had, at least, taken responsibility for the failure to adequately monitor the portfolio's activities. There would be plenty of critics who felt that his admission of "bad judgment" was the tip of the metaphorical iceberg. For now, though, Dimon was done taking blame. It was the CIO group's turn to fall on their sword.

The group's initial strategy was to blame Iksil, the London Whale himself. The standard party line was that Iksil was responsible for valuing the group's positions, so any errors were due to his actions. That argument held up briefly, but fell apart when more and more information was released, information that indicated that Iksil had argued against mis-marking the positions. Iksil then pointed at Martin-Artajo and Grout as the culprits, which began a finger-pointing circus. At that point, Iksil decided he'd played nice for long enough and began cooperating with U.S. authorities in their investigation.

*　　*　　*

The summer of 2012 was a tumultuous time for the executives at JP Morgan. The firm had to endure the embarrassment of restating their first-quarter earnings report after learning that the final tally for the loss came in at $6.2 billion. Investigators sifted through enough information – including recorded phone calls and emails – to learn that the CIO office had deliberately mis-marked prices. It was a crushing blow to Jamie Dimon, the perceived king of risk-management on Wall Street and the man who had steered the largest bank in the United States safely through the financial crisis. There was a brief, although unsuccessful, move on the part of shareholders to strip Dimon of his Chairman's title. The shareholder action was enough, however, to get Dimon's compensation cut in half; that said, he still took home $11.5 million for the year *after* his reduction in pay.

JP Morgan immediately did whatever they could do to repair their public image, and much of that focused on strengthening risk-management. The firm spent $1 billion to improve internal controls, but for some, it was a little too late. Financial regulators from both the United States and the United Kingdom swooped in and began levying fines.

The UK Financial Conduct Authority fined the bank £137,610,000 or $220 million. The United States Federal Reserve, citing the bank's "deficiencies in risk management," added another $200 million, and the U.S. Office of the Comptroller of the Currency laid on $300 million more. Then it was the Securities and Exchange Commission's turn. They focused on the fact that JP Morgan disclosed false information to the public when they failed to report accurate numbers on their quarterly earnings report. They weren't interested in who was at fault. It was the bank's responsibility to ensure the accuracy of the information. The SEC pointed out that members of the JP Morgan executive branch knew something was wrong, yet still went ahead with a May 10 earnings call and failed to explain the firm's trading losses. Those sins, in the mind of the SEC, warranted another $200 million fine.

At that point, the fines added up to $920 million, which was certainly large enough to cause a lot of grief at JP Morgan. But there was one more hit on the way, this time coming from the Commodity Futures Trading Commission. With the passage of the Dodd-Frank Wall Street Reform and Consumer Protection Act in 2010, the CFTC had acquired new powers to regulate swaps dealers. Prior to Dodd-Frank, CDS were outside their regulatory realm, but now the CFTC had acquired that authority. And since JP Morgan was a registered swaps dealer, those trades were now under the CFTC's oversight.

The CFTC determined that JP Morgan had recklessly sold massive amounts of IG9 10Y swaps during a concentrated period of time in order to affect the market on February 29th. In their quest to "defend the position," JP Morgan was charged with reckless manipulation and artificially-inflating prices. They agreed to pay $100 million to the CFTC to settle the matter once and for all, bringing the final tab for the London Whale incident to $1.02 billion.

There was another element of the new law that was problematic, but luckily for JP Morgan, it didn't warrant a fine. That element was the part of Dodd-Frank known as the Volcker Rule. Though it was not yet finalized when the CIO's subterfuge came to light, the Volcker Rule was designed to prevent banks from using federally-insured deposits for outright speculation – exactly what happened at JP Morgan. At the time, however, the rule was still in a grey area because the folks at JP Morgan were adamant that the CIO office was merely hedging the bank's assets, and not increasing risk through proprietary trading. After the official review, that contention was quickly dropped.

Jamie Dimon had been a vocal critic of Dodd-Frank and claimed the law gave regulators far too much power and influence over banks. But the London Whale incident in 2012 played right into the hands of those in favor of stricter banking rules. As a result, the Volcker Rule was amended so that portfolio hedging with federally-insured deposits was specifically banned. Ironically, the original draft of the rule would have allowed the London Whale trades, because such hedging was thought to be a systematic method to reduce risk. Iksil's actions proved otherwise, however, and the law was modified.

The London Whale episode demonstrated once again how easy it is for a person or small group of people – even at one of the world's largest and best-run banks – to hide hundreds of millions of dollars in losses. But despite the carnage, there were still winners in this rogue trading episode. Securities regulators scored a huge victory, as they got much-needed support for stronger laws. And then there were the hedge funds. In any bet, there's a winner and a loser. Boaz Weinstein won big in his bet against Iksil. Together with the other hedge funds, Saba Capital Management profited substantially from JP Morgan's failure to monitor its traders' activities. Weinstein was reported to net about $200 million for his part in the trade.

Soon after, Jamie Dimon was grilled by members of Congress in a whirlwind tour of the nation's capital. He appeared in front of the Senate on June 13, 2012, and then in front of the House on June 19. He repeatedly admitted that mistakes had been made and apologized for what he called "a tempest in a teapot." He told Congress, "If you don't acknowledge mistakes, you can't fix them and learn from them." So while it was an incredibly expensive lesson for JP Morgan, we can hope that everyone can learn from their mistakes. As a first step, Dimon ordered the CIO office to be drastically reduced and it was eventually merged with another department at JP Morgan. The bank has since added 4,000 new employees dedicated to risk monitoring and control.

*   *   *

As of this writing, the investigation into the London Whale affair is still ongoing. At its core, the investigation is about traders hiding losses, so it's hard to criticize senior management. The traders themselves were the ones responsible for perpetuating the fraud and their superiors relied on the information they provided. JP Morgan has done what it can to financially recoup from the traders. All of the employees were forced to pay back approximately two years' of compensation as dictated by their employment agreements.

Javier Martin-Artajo and Julien Grout today find themselves in an awkward situation. They both have the choice to travelling to the United States to face charges – and potentially strike a plea deal with the U.S. government – or stay somewhere where they can't be easily extradited. Both have been indicted by federal grand juries and charged with conspiracy, wire fraud, falsifying books and records, and causing JP Morgan to make false and misleading statements.

In his termination letter from JP Morgan, Martin-Artajo was accused of directing "Bruno Iksil and/or Julien Grout to show modest daily losses in the marking of the book rather than marking the book in a manner consistent with the standard policies and procedures" of the bank. Since then, Martin-Artajo remains in his native Spain at the culmination of a "long-planned" extended vacation, according to his lawyers. He turned himself in to Spanish authorities in August of 2013. Citing the fact that the events took place in the United Kingdom and his own Spanish citizenship, Martin-Artajo challenged his extradition to the United States.

Julien Grout, after being suspended from JP Morgan in July of 2012, officially resigned in December of 2012. He left London and went to his parents' weekend home in the South of France. Despite his lawyers' statement that read, "We're confident he will eventually be cleared of all wrongdoing," he, too, is fighting extradition. In the event his challenge fails, his legal strategy claims that he was just an inexperienced junior trader doing as he was told. He was, in essence, just following orders so he cannot be held liable for what happened.

Ina Drew resigned from JP Morgan on May 13, 2012. She saw an opportunity at redemption when she testified before the U.S. Senate, but her inability to fully and coherently explain the London Whale trades left Senators with a view that she had a limited understanding as to what went on under her control. At one point during her testimony, she denied having seen documents that were presented, despite the fact that Senators had proof that she had, in fact, seen the documents. Both her credibility and her ego were shattered as a result.

Following her departure from JP Morgan, she continues to claim ignorance, saying that only after resigning did she learn of the fraud, "Since my departure," she said, "I have learned of the deceptive conduct by members of the London team, and I was – and remain – deeply disappointed and saddened to learn of such conduct and the extent to which the London team let me, and the company, down." Her bank account took a substantial hit, too, as JP Morgan recouped approximately $21.5 million of back pay allowed under her employment agreement.

As for Boaz Weinstein of Saba Capital Management, the firm had a spectacular 2012, fueled by the $200 million victory over Iksil. 2013, however, was not quite as kind, with the fund ending the year down 6.75%, whereas the average credit fund returned 6.87%. The investor redemptions that followed that disappointing year saw the fund drop from $5.2 billion in assets to approximately $3.3 billion.

Which brings us to Bruno Iksil, the infamous London Whale himself. Despite being saddled with the dubious distinction of being a rogue trader, Iksil made out better than his cohorts. His termination letter stated, "You received or were aware of instructions from Javier Martin-Artajo to show modest daily losses in the marking of book rather than marking the book in a manner consistent with the standard policies and procedures of JP Morgan Chase." The fact that the firm explicitly said Iksil was acting under orders offered him the out he was looking for.

In August of 2013, U.S. prosecutors offered Iksil the opportunity avoid prosecution in exchange for his testifying against other JP Morgan employees. It was a classic prosecutorial move: offer a deal to a lower-level operative to catch the really big fish. This deal, however, had an addition bonus where Iksil would receive immunity. Prosecutors said they offered the deal to Iksil because he "sounded the alarm more than once" in regards to the illegal goings-on, but he was summarily ignored. It didn't take too long for the London Whale to understand that this was a gift, and he took it.

In the end, all of the traders involved in the London Whale fiasco met a fate similar to Captain Ahab. And just like Melville's title character, this story is about a whale destroying them all.

POWER PEG AND KNIGHT CAPITAL GROUP, 2012

Unbeknownst to the average high school student struggling with the intricacies of mathematics, that confusion was created by a late eight-century Persian named Al-Khwarizmi. Well, not exactly. He was really just the one credited with inventing the work. The man, Abu Abdullah Muhammad ibn Musa Al-Khwarizmi was born in 780 AD and was a brilliant mathematician, astronomer, and geographer. He had built upon the work of the Indian mathematician Brahmagupta and wrote a book entitled *The Compendious Book on Calculation by Completion and Balancing* in approximately 820 AD, which spread algebra – meaning "Arabic arithmetic" – to Europe. By any account, spreading algebra around the world would be a monumental achievement, but Al-Khwarizmi took it one step further.

Five years later, around 825 AD, Al-Khwarizmi made perhaps his greatest contribution to math when he described a series of repetitive mathematical calculations. When it came time to credit him with the invention, Al-Khwarizmi's name was mispronounced and the invention became known as the Algorithm. And with that malapropism, an entire field of mathematics was born. Ironically enough, once again Al-Khwarizmi was again credited for inventing the work, though he was still not the true inventor. The first algorithm goes back to the Greek mathematician named Euclid in approximately 300 B.C. who wrote what's called the Euclidean Algorithm, used to describe the process for finding the greatest common divisor of two integers.

The term algorithm that we use today refers to a set of rules for performing arithmetic, though there's no generally accepted definition. It commonly refers to any set of procedures used for solving problems or performing tasks. Informally, it's mostly used to explain a step-by-step process in either mathematics or computer programming. Think of it as a set of instructions for calculations with a number of steps that terminate at an ending point. The most common component of an algorithm is the "if-then" statement - IF the kitchen is floor is dirty, THEN you should mop it. A daily chore defined within the context of an algorithm.

Algorithms are graphically illustrated through the use of flow-charts. They show the individual steps as boxes connected to one another by arrows. A rectangular box is a single step and a diamond denotes a decision. That decision is a yes/true or no/false. Using the dirty kitchen floor algorithm, we have the question of whether or not the kitchen floor is dirty, with an arrow pointing to a diamond with a yes or no. From there, an arrow leads us to a final box telling us to either mop the floor (if the answer was yes) or to go to another chore (if the answer is no).

While the flowchart is a simplistic way of deciding whether or not to clean the kitchen floor, most algorithms are infinitely more complex, and most commonly used in computer programming. Computers perform functions using detailed algorithms that tell them what operations they should perform and under what circumstances. If a specific condition exists, then perform the specific action. The average home computer today can execute up to 100 million instructions per second, which is exponentially faster than even the most brilliant human mind. But it's important to remember that the computer doesn't think for itself. It's told exactly what to do by the programmer and then it blindly follows the exact instructions in the algorithm.

By the 1990's, stock traders realized they could harness the speed of computers and began experimenting with algorithms for executing trades. Because the computer could execute trades so much faster than any human trader, investors began using computers to program how their orders would be filled in the market. And because the computer did exactly what it was told it to do, those orders were filled precisely the way they wanted. In other words, the human became the brains while the computer was the speed. If the trade didn't pan out the way the trader had hoped, and that often happened, it wasn't because the computer did something wrong.

Algorithmic stock trading is essentially the same idea as the kitchen floor algorithm - it uses a set of rules to determine a specific action. In the case of stocks, the rules are set up to finesse trade execution. Rather than making the decision about which security to buy or sell, the algorithm decides how and when to place the order. Often, that decision involves splitting large stock order into multiple smaller orders to reduce visibility in the market. In other words, executing smaller trades so that other traders can't see what a large investor is trying to do. In its simplest form, algorithmic stock trading involves the typical if-then statement: IF the stock price hits $50.00 a share, THEN sell 1,000 shares every five minutes for a total of two hours.

As the size of institutional investor's orders grew in size and electronic stock trading exploded, so, too, did the use of algorithmic trading. But it all goes back to the one firm which pioneered the algorithmic trading bandwagon - Knight Capital Group.

*   *   *

In an industry littered with generations of old-line firms, Knight Capital Group was the new kid on the block. Founded in 1995 by Kenneth Pasternak and Walter Raquet, Knight was not headquartered on fabled Wall Street, but across the river in Jersey City. It owed both its inception and rapid growth to the NASDAQ stock market, a growth that was spurred by the technological advancements of the 1990s.

In 1992, Raquet and Pasternak were both working at a firm called Spear, Leeds & Kellogg. As Raquet looked around the trading floor, he was struck by the fact so much of the buying and selling was dependent on traders and salespeople quoting markets over the phone, despite recent advancements in technology. With the Internet suddenly shifting into reality, information on stock prices was available in real-time and available to anyone who cared to access it. Raquet knew there was a better way for the market-makers at Spear to operate.

Market-makers are the traders who provide liquidity in the stock market. When a customer is trying to either buy or sell, the market-maker will show them a bid or an offer and take the opposite side of the trade, regardless of whether the market-maker is an actual buyer or seller. In the days when floor traders ruled the New York Stock Exchange, the market-makers were referred to as "specialists," and they were charged with matching buy and sell orders, while taking long and short positions to make a little for themselves. With the advent of the computer and its impact on the financial markets, technology was beginning to rule the day. It was no longer necessary for brokers and traders to meet face-to-face in order to execute a stock, and they certainly didn't need to be standing on a stock exchange trading floor.

POWER PEG AND KNIGHT CAPITAL GROUP, 2012

Raquet had the technological insight to see that the old exchange model was outdated and it would inevitably be replaced by computerized trading. It was a revolutionary way to think at the time, given that stock traders had been meeting in person since the days of the Buttonwood tree in 1792, when they originally formed the New York Stock Exchange. Raquet wanted to be at the forefront of the movement, and in 1992, he approached his colleague Pasternak, one of the top traders at Spear, and pitched the idea. Both men immediately agreed to work together to create the next-generation stock market-making firm.

They reasoned that once the general public had access to real-time stock quotes via the Internet, individuals would begin self-directing their own stock transactions. Stock buyers wouldn't need the services of a massive investment bank, and, with all of the discount brokers popping up, individuals finally had the ability to gain low-cost market access. Today, there are countless online discount brokers who offer investment services, but in 1992, people didn't consider the idea very realistic. The pair submitted a business plan to Spear, Leeds & Kellogg for a group focusing on on-line brokers and Peter Kellogg agreed with them. However, the old-school senior people at SLK didn't see their vision exactly the same way. Instead, Kellogg agreed to let Pasternak and Raquet put their business plan together and take whichever employees they wanted with them. It was an incredibly generous exit offer.

The following year, they approached Lawrence Waterhouse, the Chairman of the discount brokerage firm called Waterhouse Securities, and proposed the idea. This time the idea struck a chord. However, Waterhouse knew his firm was too small to support a market-making firm on their own. Rather than rejecting the idea outright, Waterhouse suggested that the team bring together five other discount brokers and create a stand-alone firm owned by the discount brokers.

Raquet and Pasternak took the idea and ran with it. They called their new firm Roundtable Partners, a reference to King Arthur and his fabled Knights of the Round Table, where each knight sharing an equal seat around the table with the king. The new business model would have that same egalitarian concept, with each brokerage firm sharing equally in the ownership. In March 1995, Roundtable Partners was launched with a consortium of 20 different discount brokers, far more than the original five had hoped for.

They created a subsidiary called Knight Securities in July of that year, which became the market-making arm of Roundtable Partners for both the NASDAQ and the Over-the-Counter (OTC) stocks. Then, they acquired a firm named Trimark Securities, which operated on both the New York Stock Exchange and the American Stock Exchange. That acquisition, paired with their existing presence in NASDAQ and OTC, positioned Knight in all of the major U.S. stock exchanges. With 75 employees and $17 million in capital, Knight began making-markets in 2,000 individual stocks, putting them squarely in the trailing position of the 88th largest market-maker on the NASDAQ exchange.

The real beauty of the business, at least from Knight's perspective, was that they often got paid on both sides of the transaction. Whereas TD Ameritrade might be sending a buy order for a particular stock, Charles Schwab might be sending a sell order for the same stock at the same time. Knight, being the market-maker, filled the orders themselves - buying on the bid-side and selling on the offered-side and thus, capturing the bid/offer spread. With the sheer volume of all the discount broker trades going thorough their system, Knight was often buying and selling the same stock at the same time, making the bid-offer spread and essentially taking no risk. The business of electronic stock market-making became pretty simple; it was all about numbers and volume. The more volume a firm could run through their books, the more money they would make with the computers were doing the majority of the work. And, even better, those computers never asked for raises or took coffee breaks. Raquet and Pasternak clearly had a winner.

By 1997, Knight had grown to become the single largest market-maker of NASDAQ stocks, benefitting directly from individuals executing their own trades online without having to call their broker. And just as the founders hoped, Knight was the innovator in low-cost stock market execution, positioned right at the epicenter of the Internet explosion. The firm became the trusted intermediary for America's retail stock brokers and perhaps most importantly, the customers loved Knight. 99.3% of all client orders were executed in under a second, which meant that investors were almost guaranteed the market price when they wanted to buy or sell. No waiting. It might seem like second nature these days, but back then, it was revolutionary. And Knight became very popular – they were executing between 40% and 50% of all U.S. on-line retail stock order flow – that is, almost half of all mom and pop electronic stock trades were going through Knight.

With that kind of volume also came money. Lots and lots of money. The firm was a money-making machine sprouting out cash. Forget about the traders at Solomon Brothers and Drexel Burnham in the 1980s or even a Goldman Sachs partner in the 1990s, they made a pittance compared to the money being made by Knight's traders. Senior trading managers were making between $15 million and $26 million a year. That's in one year! And it was because they took home at least 5% of their group's net revenue as their compensation. Combine that with Knight stock appreciation and top traders were making upwards of $25 million annually, and even trading assistants, the newbies on the trading desks, were pocketing close to a cool million each year.

Then in July of 1998, Knight used those three little words that investors love to hear – Initial Public Offering – and raised an immediate

$145 million more in capital. Within six months after the firm went public, its market capitalization soared from $725 million to $2 billion; by the end of 1999 – a timeframe of just eighteen months – that value ballooned to a staggering $8 billion, making Pasternak briefly a billionaire. The massive growth was fueled by the stock trading business, and with it, most of the credit going to Pasternak as a stock trading genius. As Pasternak became the public face of the company, it fostered deep tension between himself and Raquet, who still considered himself the brains behind the operation. After all, it was his idea in the beginning. But money talks on Wall Street and good ideas come a dime a dozen. Accolades are often reserved for those who are making money today, not the ones who had good ideas yesterday.

That's not to say that Knight didn't have some problems too. Anytime money is involved in the exchange of goods or services, there's almost always someone who finds a way to exploit the loopholes. When you're talking about the opportunity to make millions of dollars – with smart people overseeing money going back and forth – it's not too surprising that some people were looking to skim some off the top. There were more than a few scandals that rocked Knight over the years.

For starters, there were plenty of rumors at other firms that their colleagues at Knight were engaged in front-running. Front-running is when a trader jumps in front of a customer order to buy or sell a stock. In other words, the trader sees an order come in from an investor and immediately submits the same order before putting through the client's order. It's illegal, but it doesn't mean some smart minds can't find a way around those regulations.

First, because there was such massive volume going through their trading books, the guys at Knight were in a perfect position to make money from front-running - they saw almost everything going on in the market. Knight traders not only saw when the big customers were buying and selling, but they saw the size of the trades and at what price the client wanted to buy or sell. It doesn't take a good trader to capitalize on that kind of insider information; and make a financial killing in the process. Many top executives and traders were well aware of the front-running at Knight in the 1990s and referred to it as "a racket."

There were plenty of ways to front-run, you just had to know how to do it, especially in a way that didn't outwardly violate NASD rules. First, Knight traders routinely drove up the opening prices of IPO stocks on their first day of trading. Before a new IPO stock opened for trading, traders saw the pre-market buy orders coming into their books - customer orders like "buy on the open." Now, if the IPO stock price was set at $25.00 a share and a trader sees millions of shares trying to buy on the open, they clearly didn't want to sell their customers at $25.00 a share. Instead, they made sure the stock price opened at higher levels. Traders bid up IPO stock prices in the pre-market until the price reached a point where it seemed like a good level to sell, say $40.00 a share. When the stock opened at $40.00, Knight traders would sell the stock on the opening to their unwary customers. Then, at the artificially inflated opening price, they oversold the stock and short-sold it. As the opening buyers disappeared and the stock price drifted lower, they'd buy back their shorts at wildly deflated prices. Laughing all the way to the bank. It's nothing too complicated – the same "pump and dump" scams have been used in the past – but who would have thought making money from opening IPO orders would be so easy?

Another front-running scam was equally simple and equally effective for making money. It involved *not filling* a customer's order unless the trader was guaranteed to make a profit. Regulations at the time allowed market-makers to delay filling customer orders, even if the stock was trading at the level the customer wanted. Traders would routinely place orders in a "pending file" and waited. Any stock order that was placed in the "pending file" had no obligation of being filled. When the stock price moved past the order price and the trader was assured of a profit, he'd fill the order and send a trade confirmation. Again, it's nothing fancy or complex. It made money for the traders, and that was the name of the game.

John Hewitt, an executive brought in from Goldman Sachs to become President of Knight Capital Group, caught wind of the front-running rumors and discovered there were plenty of less-than-moral activities going on. He called Pasternak and said, "We have a problem. Let's fire these guys immediately."

It was a little too late. The National Association of Securities Dealers (NASD), the regulatory authority at the time, had already been looking into the rumors. Ken Pasternak, together with the head of Knight's Institutional Sales Desk John Leighton, were under investigation for failure to supervise the trading activities of Joseph Leighton, who happened to be John's brother and one of four Leighton brothers who worked at Knight. Though front-running was pretty widespread at Knight, the NASD only went after the worst offenders, and Joseph was found to be involved in all kinds of fraudulent trading activities during his days at Knight.

In 2005, Pasternak, together with John Leighton, would receive fines of $100,000 each for failure to supervise the trading activities of Joseph Leighton. Joseph was forced to pay more than $4 million in fines and received perhaps the harshest punishment the NASD could hand down: He was barred from the securities industry. Pasternak and John Leighton, however, fought the SEC in court and were later cleared of any wrongdoing. When the final numbers were tallied, as a firm, Knight paid in excess of $79 million in fines resulting from the front-running charges.

*　*　*

In the end, the practice of front-running by individual traders was not eradicated by either new rules or new regulations. Instead, it was done by taking the human trader out of the equation. Around this time, technology had eliminated much of the ability of the human trader to front-run investor orders. Putting together buyer and seller was no longer being done by human market-markers. Rather, it was being done by matching engines inside computer black boxes.

With the advent of computerized order placing systems, institutional investors had new ways to disguise their market intentions when submitting large orders. All of a sudden, the electronic trading facilities had created new ways of placing orders, and as a result, the major stock exchanges were beginning to lose favor with big investors. Investor orders were migrating to the new electronic exchanges.

The average investor has probably heard of the big name U.S. stock exchanges – the NYSE, the AMEX, and the NASDAQ – and might have a passing knowledge of an international exchange or two. If they dabble in penny stocks, then OTC and the Pink Sheets are something they're familiar with. But back ten years ago, 85% of all U.S. stock trading still occurred on the NYSE. Today, there are 13 different public stock exchanges, and that's just the tip of the stock trading iceberg. Exchange names include: BATS, Direct Edge, International Securities Exchange (ISE), and the National Stock Exchange (NSX), and even the recently publicized Investors Exchange (IEX)[8]. These days, the ubiquitous Wall Street of the stock market isn't in downtown Manhattan anymore. It's in New Jersey. The ISE and the NSX

---

[8] As of this writing, the IEX is currently a "dark pool" and has applied to become an exchange.

are located, of all places, in Jersey City, New Jersy. BATS is located right next door in Weehawken, New Jersey. When you buy or sell a stock on the NYSE, the trade doesn't actually occur in the old NYSE building. The computer matching engine is located further up Route 17, in Mahwah, New Jersey. And the exchanges are all, more or less, computer-driven. No floor traders need apply.

Outside of trading on an exchange, there are numerous banks which have in-house trade matching in ominous sounding "dark pools," of which there are 50 around the world. Dark pools aren't quite as secret as their name suggests. The dark in their name is, on one level, because no one is supposed to know what's happening inside of them. That is, the details of those markets aren't available to the general public. They are actually a hold-over from the old concept known as "upstairs trading," which was nothing more than a method of hiding large trades from the prying eyes of the specialists on the floor of the exchange.

Suppose a large institutional investor didn't want to send their order down to the exchange floor and risk someone front-running it. They knew their order was large enough that if the size got out, it would move the market. Upstairs trading was a way of keeping those orders insulated from the trading floor; an institutional investor or a major client negotiated a purchase or sale directly with a securities dealer. These days it's called trading in a dark pool.

It's important to note, that there's nothing illegal about dark pools, despite the connotations implied by their name. Plenty of banks run these quasi-secret sales outlets. There are approximately 45 dark pools around the country that compete with the 13 public exchanges; Crossfinder, the Credit Suisse dark pool, is the largest and it trades somewhere north of 132 million shares a day. Goldman Sachs would dispute Crossfinder's dominance by claiming that their Sigma X dark pool is really the largest. Barclay's dark pool trading venue is called LX and claims to trade 110 million shares a day. All in all, there's no way to be sure who's the largest since the banks publish their own volume numbers in their own way, however, it's estimated that dark pools account for anywhere from 14% to 40% of all U.S. stock trading on any given day.

Many of the same problems which plagued Knight in the late 1990s ended up resurfacing again in the early 2000s. At first, with electronic trading, there was no way to finesse large orders in and out of the market. The risk of a human trader front-running the order just resurfaced in electronic front-running. Instead of humans doing it, HFT (High Frequency Trading) firms were teaching computers to do it. Institutional investors were once again not happy; they were being outgunned by computerized traders and they needed a solution to hide their orders from the prying eyes of HFT traders. Once again, they needed a way to execute large trades without simultaneously moving the market against them. To solve this dilemma, the folks at Knight turned to a Persian mathematician who had written a treatise centuries ago about repetitive calculations - the algorithm.

Algorithmic order execution was designed for the most part to help large-volume traders spread a single transaction out over an extended period of time and across multiple exchanges. One of the more popular algorithmic executions is called the parent-and-child order. Say an institutional customer wants to buy 1 million shares of a particular stock and sends that order through an algorithmic execution system. The entire order – the full million shares – becomes the parent order.

From that point, the algorithm's parameters are programmed by the investor. The algorithm will search all of the possible markets – exchanges, dark pools, any possible outlet for trading the stock – and send out smaller buy orders at the best price it can locate. These are the child orders, and there's no trail that leads back to the investor – and the single parent order.

The size of individual child orders and the pricing details are determined by the investor, as is the length of time to keep the algorithm active. The algorithm executes the order within the customer's parameters until it's filled or the time limit expires, whichever comes first.

It didn't take long for smaller-scale investors to catch on to the benefits of algorithmic trading, and the new order-placing strategy became very popular with them too. Other types of algorithmic orders that were created were called peg orders. In one type of peg order, the customer dictates a price above or below the best bid or offer in the market and "pegs" his order to that price. For example, a 1/8 peg order to buy places the order 1/8 of a point below the bid price. If the bid was $25.375, then the peg buy order would be $25.25.

Modifications included a "mid-price peg," in which the peg price is the average of the best bid and the best offer. Alternatively, a "peg best" places the bid or offer as always the best in the market. If a better bid or offer comes in, then the algorithm is programmed to automatically beat that price by a set increment.

At Knight, the first algorithmic peg order routing system was called Power Peg, a system that was originally developed in-house to execute parent-and-child orders. Technology at the time allowed Power Peg to send thousands of buy and sell orders to the exchanges every second. At the time, Power Peg was placing orders in ways that no human trader could ever hope to.

The system was keyed by a flag in Knight's computer system. When the flag was up, it meant that there was an active parent order in effect and Power Peg kept sending the child orders to the various trading outlets. As orders were filled, a tracking function counted the number of child executions. Once the size of the individual child orders equaled the size of the parent order, the parent order was filled and the flag went down. When the flag was down,

Power Peg stopped sending orders. That fact would become very important in its infamous reign as a rogue trader.

Today, algorithmic trading systems are even more advanced. Many are programed with a fail-safe provisions: including automatic shutdowns that stop the process if the price moves outside its normal trading range. It's a way to prevent unintended trade executions at prices the customer never intended, but in the late 1990s and early 2000s, firms had not yet developed this technology. It was something that no one considered important at the time. As such, Power Peg was not designed with an automatic shutdown feature. And that would later become a very costly design flaw.

*　*　*

Computerized stock trading wasn't the only change in the stock market at this time. On April 9, 2001, a new rule was passed by the Securities and Exchange Commission (SEC) called NMS Rule 612. The SEC had concluded that tick sizes in 1/8 of a point were artificially widening the spread between the bid and offer prices. They determined that it led to excessive profit-taking by market-makers like Knight (no kidding!). As a result, the SEC mandated that the stock market move to decimal pricing.

Foreign markets had long been using the decimal system, with tick sizes of 1/100 of a point or 0.01. Overnight, U.S. stocks went from a system of a 20 1/8 bid and 20 1/4 offer, to quoted with a 20.13 bid and 20.15 offer. Studies showed that investors could save more than $1 billion annually from narrower spreads; and they did. Market-makers, however, saw their profits collapse. And because Knight was at the top of the market-maker food chain, they were the hardest hit from the rule change. The new rule even required market-makers to execute some orders for no profit at all. Essentially, it meant they were forced to do some trades out of the goodness of their hearts. Not the typical creed on Wall Street.

In a desperate attempt to right the sinking ship, Knight switched to a hybrid market-making model in hopes of damming the flood of cash draining from the company. They allowed electronic trading for some institutional customers, while they continued traditional human market-making for other customers. But there was no stopping such a fundamental change in the market, profits continued to decline and Knight's business model basically collapsed. Knight President John Hewitt immediately realized the gravity of the situation: "It took zero time for the economics to fall off the cliff," he said of the new SEC rule, "The traders were unable to make money anymore. The whole compensation model fell. We were sitting there losing three million dollars a day." Many former Knight traders still contend that the change to decimalization was the ultimate cause of Knight's demise.

Throughout 2001, Kenny Pasternak was often heard complaining about his job, saying how much he hated the work and wanted to quit. But as he'd been there from the beginning, it wasn't an easy decision to just pack up and leave. He no longer saw Knight as a just a business that he was building, it had become somewhat of a family to him. But the reality was settling in, and one employee observed, "Pasternak had lost all drive to be the CEO."

At the end of that year, the board formally asked Pasternak for his resignation, which he gladly submitted. "I was already looking for an opportunity to retire," he said. His forced retirement left the firm's traders wondering about their future, as well as the future of the firm they worked for.

In an attempt to return to profitability, Knight turned to a business strategy based on high volume. Because the profits they made from each trade were so low, they felt that more trading volume would offset the declining revenues. They expanded their strategy to pay money to the online brokerage firms for their business, a practice that became known as "paying for order flow." Large retail brokers – firms like TD Ameritrade and Scottrade, for example – received payments from Knight in exchange for sending more business to the struggling firm. From Knight's perspective, it was worth the cost. After all, they made the bulk of their money as a market-maker - collecting the spread between the bid and the offer, even though that spread had narrowed considerably.

The plan worked, to a degree, and Knight saw an increase in trading volume. But it came at a tangential cost, namely the firm's computer systems and servers were having problems keeping up with the trading activity. It got so bad that the computer system was going down almost on a daily basis, and the firm knew they had to change their business model again – and build up their technology. The computer systems would begin doing more of the market-making activity, and with it, they'd be able to cut staff and reduce costs.

The new grand plan at Knight was to cut as much of the trading staff as possible, thereby saving millions of dollars. The firm had, at the time, several hundred full-time traders and they wanted to cut that number to less than 100. The massive decrease in traders would be offset through computer automation of their market-making functions. That way, they could squeeze much more productivity from the traders they retained. The plan was put into action in March of 2002 with the first announcement of an 8% cut in staff.

The next step was hiring a new Chief Executive Officer to replace Pasternak. The board of directors decided on Tom Joyce, a well-known industry veteran from Merrill Lynch. He was a Harvard graduate who excelled in sports as a student and that athletic prowess was so much a part of his persona that he had a reputation for hiring only Ivy League athletes to work for him.

Joyce was a CEO who preferred to look at the big picture and develop relationships with clients, especially during rounds of golf, dinners, and meetings directly with the clients. "He was always out with clients," recalled one former Knight employee. Joyce's plan was to take Knight away from the cowboy culture that existed since its founding and turn it into a corporate environment. His vision was a miniature version of Merrill Lynch, the firm he'd been hired away from. All in all, it was an undertaking that would require a ton of detailed work.

The first step Joyce took was to change the firm's compensation system. He shifted to the standard big investment bank salary-and-bonus model, with discretionary bonuses decided by the new managers that Joyce himself had hand-picked. Traders who had been with the firm for many years were less than pleased and many old-time Knight employees felt that Joyce had sent too many experienced personnel packing; traders who had proven themselves over the years.

Within a year, however, it looked like Joyce's strategy was working. In 2002, whereas the firm lost $42.2 million for the year, in 2003, that loss had been replaced with a $38.5 million profit.

Buoyed by the sudden financial reversal, he retired many of the old Knight electronic execution systems and bought new firms with new trading technology, including a new order routing system called Smart Market Access Routing System (SMARS). Like Power Peg before it, SMARS was set up to receive parent orders and then send out the smaller child orders to external trading platforms. The system was up-to-date, faster, more reliable, and could compare prices between more than 50 different trading venues within fractions of a second. Whereas Power Peg was inconceivably fast in its day, performing several thousand transactions per second, it was now the equivalent to a horse and buggy. SMARS was capable of executing as many as 2 million orders per second. Ultimately, that mind-boggling speed would become the metaphorical straw that broke the camel's back.

Power Peg was decommissioned in 2003. It was turned off, yet remained on Knight's servers. It's a common practice by many computer programmers; oftentimes rather than delete old programs, they'll simply disable them. The firm had always intended to delete Power Peg altogether, but for some reason they never got around to it.

Regardless of why the program was never erased, it's the equivalent of a retired executive who is allowed to keep an office in the building, despite the fact that he doesn't really do anything anymore. And just like that aging figurehead, Power Peg still had its brains intact. It was still functional, all it needed was to be told what to do.

The next step was building algorithmic trading for their own market-making purposes. By hiring a group of quant programmers, they were able to develop all of their market-making algorithms internally, effectively the first step in eliminating the bulk of their human traders. Joyce flipped the switch in the second quarter of 2005 and the firm went completely automated.

Joyce's next step was a corporate acquisition spree in an attempt to diversify the firm away from solely market-making in stocks. Joyce acquired Attain, an electronic communications firm, in May 2005, and followed that up with the acquisition of Direct Trading Institutional, a firm that specialized in providing institutional investors with trading executions at a low cost.

The buying continued in 2006, with the acquisition of Hotspot FX in January, which gave Knight's institutional clients electronic access to the foreign exchange markets. In October of that year, Atlanta-based Value Bond was brought under the Knight umbrella to jump-start the firm into electronic trading in the fixed-income markets. In 2007, he purchased EdgeTrade, a stock broker and software developer. Then, he acquired Libertas Holdings in 2008, as well as a company called Oasis, which had algorithms designed to trade stock pairs - allowing clients to trade the spread between two or more related securities in 2009. Three other acquisitions brought in state-of-the-art algorithms for trading, Urban Financial Group, Astor Asset Management, and Kellogg Capital Markets in 2010.

By 2012, the firm would have 40 market-makers and 185 computer programmers, compared to June of 2002 when the firm had 260 market-makers, all human traders, and five programmers. All of this technology – new and old – was housed in Knight's data center, located on the fourth floor of their Jersey City headquarters. Included in this technology stockpile were eight separate high-speed servers that ran the firm's computer trading and execution programs, and each server was responsible for trading a different group of NYSE stocks. The firm had been completely transformed into a high-tech computer automated franchise.

*   *   *

In what should have been a wake-up call for everyone in the financial markets, the Dow Jones Industrial Average (DJIA) posted its largest intra-day loss in history on May 6, 2010. Oftentimes, the average person assumes that a drop of that magnitude is caused by some seismic event in the markets. Things like a bank default or a major financial crisis are typical culprits. But not in this case. No, that massive drop was due to an algorithmic high-frequency trading error that occurred within the timespan of minutes.

By 2010, the algorithms being used in HFT accounted for as much of 70% of all stock trading. They were incredibly sophisticated and computers were now placing orders in the market at incredibly high speeds. The human trader was running on autopilot and it was a bomb just waiting to go off.

On that faithful day of May 6, 2010, investors started the day concerned about the looming European debt crisis, especially what was happening in Greece. At 2:42 PM, the DJIA was down 300 points. Then, within five minutes, the index had plummeted down another 600 points. Seconds later, the market hit the day's nadir and was down a full 1000 points on the day. By the close of trading, it had managed to claw its way back slightly, posting a 600 point drop at 4:00 PM in New York. About $1 trillion in market capitalization had been erased by the day's trading, and it still remains the largest one-day decline in the Dow's history. The event came to be known as the Flash Crash.

The SEC, together with the Commodity Futures Trading Commission, launched an immediate investigation to figure out how the U.S. stock market could possibly lose $1 trillion in the space of a couple of hours. What they found was, in fact, that it had only taken twenty minutes for an algorithm to bring the financial world to its knees. According to the agencies' joint report, at 2:32 PM, a mutual fund named Waddell & Reed had begun using an algorithm to execute a standard parent-child sell order for 75,000 E-Minis futures contracts worth approximately $4.1 billion. E-Minis are futures contracts that trade on the Chicago Mercantile Exchange and each individual contract is worth 50 times the value of the S&P 500 stock index. They're often used as a hedge by institutional investors to protect their portfolios from declining markets, without having to sell their individual stocks. On May 6th, the European debt crisis was causing them enough worry enough to want to hedge their holdings.

The traders at Waddell & Reed instructed their algorithm to send sell child orders as large as 9% of the trading volume calcu-lated over the previous minute. In other words, the program was supposed to sell the $4.1 billion parent order piece-meal, not more than 9% of the trading volume posted every minute. However, the traders made a tragic mistake, they forgot to set both a time and price parameter, so the algorithm simply unloaded the shares as quickly as it could, without regard to price. Then, with no pre-determined time for the algorithm to stop selling, it continued executing orders as the market dropped.

Other firms had their own algorithms running to purchase the E-Minis contracts that Waddell & Reed was selling but, as the market dropped, they immediately switched to selling, which sent the market into a free-fall. And because it was all computerized, the trades were taking place at a rapid-fire pace, Waddell & Reed's algorithm interpreted that as a need to sell even faster. Within 14 seconds, a total of 27,000 contracts were traded. With the price of the E-Minis accelerating downward, selling moved to other exchanges as investors started selling their actual stock holdings, and, by then, the panic had spread throughout the entire U.S. stock market.

In the end, the event was blamed on a computer malfunction, but remember, the algorithm was done exactly what it was told to do, to the letter. There was no minimum price limit and no timeframe set; the algorithm was simply following instructions. For all of the advancements we've made in technology, there is still no computer anywhere that possesses the human survival instinct that tells it to stop selling when it's creating a panic in the market.

Following the Flash Crash, many exchanges allowed trades to be cancelled as a way to helping their members starve off the massive losses they'd sustained. The New York Stock Exchange, for example, cancelled all trades that were 30% or more away from the price at the start of the trading day. As a result, many market participants lived to tell about the Flash Crash and were elated. Just as many, however, were unhappy; those who had benefitted from the free-fall.

Additionally, two new rules were put in place to govern securities trading. Circuit breakers were required to halt trading if the market experienced what were labeled as "significant price fluctuations."

Called limit-up/limit-down bands, the rule stated that if a stock moved up or down by 10% or more during a five-minute period, there would be a mandated pause in trading for five minutes. It was something of a time-out for traders, a period for them to collect their thoughts and think about what they were doing before potentially wreaking havoc on the financial markets.

The second new rule which was instituted by the SEC. Rule 15c3-5, also known as the Market Access Rule, dictated that the exchange would have algorithms in place designed to ensure the integrity of their computerized systems. It also required that broker-dealers implement their own risk management controls to block erroneous orders from reaching exchanges in the first place. The rule was written to specifically protect the markets from the type of rogue algorithmic computer trading that created the Flash Crash, but as we have seen so many times before, more regulations don't often equal more safety in the financial markets.

*   *   *

In the year following the Flash Crash, the NYSE began discussing the creation of a new retail stock trading platform for its members. In July of 2012, the exchange finally received approval from the SEC to establish the new Retail Liquidity Program (RLP). The basic idea was that orders from retail investors – average individuals who buy and sell stocks, as opposed to large institutions – would be directed into a single dark pool, run by the NYSE with the new pricing rule that allowed stocks to be quoted with as little as $.001 increments. If market-makers thought the old one cent pricing was bad, the new increment was going to be 1/10 of a penny.

In the RLP dark pool, member firms could bid and offer for the retail orders that were submitted. The result for investors would be, at least in theory, better prices. If retail investors didn't like the one cent bid/offer spread for a stock, they had the ability to transact somewhere in the middle. The promise of a smaller bid/offer spread for individual investors was touted as a huge step forward in the investing world. Market-makers, like Knight, were adamantly opposed. They felt that the creation of this special dark pool was solely an attempt to move trading back to the exchange. What's more, because price increments were less than a penny, market-making spreads were being gutted even further. Going from 1/8 of a point to one cent was bad enough, now they couldn't even make a penny!

But the decision was made and keeping profits high at market-maker firms wasn't the top priority of anyone else in the industry. This time, the NYSE clearly favored keeping volume on the exchange over the profits of its members. The RLP dark pool was set to come into existence on the morning of August 1, 2012.

In anticipation of the new program, the NYSE had been working on the software specifications with its members to handle the orders. There was a new trading location to send orders and new rules for market trading. The software specifications were sent out as far back as December 2011.

Despite their misgivings about the new dark pool, Knight executives were even more wary of losing customers. They didn't want to give their customers any reason whatsoever to trade elsewhere, and if that meant smaller market-making spreads, so be it. Knight's programmers worked on the upgrade code to their SMARS order handling software and updated the execution programs to accommodate RLP orders. Then, when the new program was formally approved, they still had a few weeks to finalize everything.

Ordinarily, when a new computer update is installed, it's tested repeatedly to make sure that there are no bugs. Knight, being a technology oriented firm, constantly updated and modified their systems. The testing process could take weeks or even months; the more important the system upgrade, the longer the testing process. And when you're talking about one of the world's largest financial markets, there's little room for error.

On July 27, 2012, the IT department was convinced they had a working version of the software upgrade and prepared for migrating the software into the SMARS system. RLP was going live on August 1, 2012 and Knight had to be open for business. On July 31, the night before RLP went live, Knight's SMARS programmers began loading the new software on to the servers.

I cannot speak from first-hand experience about the intricacies of loading a new trade execution system onto a computer server. It was late at night, so perhaps that had something to do with it. Whatever the reason, the updated software was only loaded on to seven of the firm's eight servers. At first glance, it doesn't seem like such a critical error.

In hindsight, it was disastrous. It's common practice in the industry to have a second IT person check the work of the first, just to make sure that everything was installed properly. Knight's IT department was top-notch so perhaps they didn't always see a reason to double-check their work. They were experienced in this sort of thing, that is, they handled over 100 software updates every year and those updates generally worked flawlessly, so there wasn't any apparent need to double-check their work. As one Knight executive later said, "The IT guys were arrogant."

In the ancient Greek tragedy, the concept of hubris is a commonly a contributing factor to the downfall of the tragic hero. It's the hero's hubris – his belief in his own infallibility – that prevents him from seeing what's right in front of him, namely that he is bringing on his own demise through his actions. Where the story of Knight is a tragedy, on some levels, Knight is a tragic hero and the hubris of the IT personnel is a tragic flaw.

At 8:00 the next morning, the pre-market orders began to accumulate on the SMARS system. But something was wrong, and SMARS started sending out an automated error message to a group of 97 Knight employees. "Power Peg disabled," the message read. "Power Peg disabled" over and over again. The market was opening in 90 minutes, though Power Peg was decommissioned nine years earlier, it wasn't even supposed to be operational. Perhaps those 97 employees had never even heard of Power Peg, but Power Peg had just woken up from its nine year slumber.

At 9:30 AM, the market opened. Normally, it might not matter that new software was not loaded correctly on one server, but this time it did. Back when the Power Peg system was operational, there was a flag that told Power Peg when the parent orders had been filled. When the flag was up, Power Peg kept sending child orders to the various exchanges. When the flag was down, Power Peg stopped sending orders. As it happened, the programmers had recycled the old flag for the new RLP update. As soon as that flag was up, Power Peg miraculously came back to life, it was a signal for Power Peg to start trading again. The orders that went through the other seven servers worked fine, but for the orders assigned to the eighth server, Power Peg took the reins and started doing what it was supposed to do.

As the orders came in, Power Peg began executing them, taking the main order as a parent and sending out child orders across the exchanges. 212 premarket orders came into that eighth server and Power Peg was doing what it was programmed to do: buying on the offer and selling on the bid, then repeating the process endlessly. As long as the flag remained up, Power Peg kept going. And because there was nothing to turn the flag off, Power Peg never stopped. It was buying and selling 140 NYSE stocks and ETFs and executing 2,400 transactions a minute.

At that frenetic pace, it didn't take long for traders on the floor of the NYSE to notice that something was up. Within the first minutes of trading, volume was 12% higher than normal. After a couple of minutes more, NYSE stocks had traded the equivalent of 30 days' worth of volume. And Power Peg was just getting started.

You might think the new rules established after the Flash Crash – the rules specifically designed to prevent a rogue algorithm from doing exactly what was being done – would have kicked in. But the circuit breakers weren't designed for massive trading volume, they were designed for large price swings. The same was true for the limit up/limit down bands. They weren't triggered either, for the same reason. Those protections only came into play when stock prices were moving up or down by 10% or more and that wasn't happening. Power Peg was massively buying on the offered side and equally selling on the bid side. The stocks really weren't moving outside of their trading ranges.

Then, what about the internal risk controls at Knight? Nearly all of the trading accounts at Knight had limits in place to auto-matically trigger a shut-down if certain thresholds were reached. That is to say, there were risk limits in place for every trading account except for one: the error account.

The error account was the trading account designated for the trading mistakes generated in those other accounts. As such, it never dawned on anyone at Knight that they needed stop-gap measures to shut down the error account. It just didn't seem necessary. Since Power Peg's resurrection wasn't a part of the firm's normal trading protocol, all of the Power Peg trades were automatically sent to the error account.

At 9:34, NYSE computer technicians traced the massive volume spike back to Knight. They found that 20% of the entire NYSE trading volume was being driven by the Electronic Trading Group (ETG) at Knight. Duncan Niederauer, the CEO of the NYSE, immediately tried to call Tom Joyce to inform him about it. Joyce, however, wasn't in the office. He was at home recovering from knee surgery.

That information was then routed to Knight's Chief Information Officer who, upon hearing the news, immediately gathered together the firm's top IT people and headed to the fourth-floor data center to figure out what exactly was happening. Ideally, this was the perfect time to flip the kill switch that is *de rigueur* in most trading systems today. But again, they didn't have that option, because no one in the market had ever installed them at this point in time.

After nearly twenty minutes – all the while Power Peg was freely trading – the Knight technicians decided that the problem was most likely something to do with the new code they'd installed - a pretty standard first response for programmers when something goes wrong with a new software update. Because they knew the old version worked fine, it made sense to their algorithmic brains that reinstalling the old system would solve the problem. IF the new system is acting up, THEN go back to the old one. As it turned out, it was the worst thing they could have done.

Within a couple of minutes, the techs had successfully removed all of the new RLP algorithms from the SMARS update. However, that action didn't turn off the flag that was telling Power Peg to buy and sell; Power Peg just kept going. But now, the updates were turned off at all of the other seven servers, and not just server number eight. Power Peg jumped in to fill that void and was now was running on all eight servers simultaneously. Buying on the offer, selling on the bid.

It wasn't until 9:58 that the programmers located the problem. They immediately shut Power Peg down, but not before the algorithm had done an incredible amount of damage. For the time-span of a full 28 minutes, it's easy to criticize the group for the delay.

But a former Knight executive explained it with the following analogy: Imagine you have a young child who has locked himself in a bathroom. He is inside screaming for help. You have a large ring of keys, all of which look the same and one will unlock the door. As you go through the process trying one key after another, the child continues to cry and scream from the other side, with the shrieks growing in intensity. When you fit the seventh key in the lock, the door opened and lets the child free.

That's precisely what happened with Knight's IT staff. They tried all of the typical fixes to solve the problem, methodically one after the other, all of the fixes that had worked in the past. It took six attempts at choosing the wrong fix before they found the right one. Just like the algorithm they were trying to shut down. IF this fix doesn't work, THEN try the next most likely solution. Repeat as needed.

At 9:59, George Sohos, the head of the head of market-making, called Joyce at his home to alert him as to what had happened and reassured him that they'd solved the problem. Surprisingly, no one had thought to call Joyce until the situation was resolved. The bleeding had stopped. Power Peg's career as a stock trading algorithm had officially ended – never to be allowed on the trading floor again. But they'd lost a lot of blood in the process. Trading volume on the NYSE was 364 million shares during the first half-hour that morning. The typical volume for that timeframe was only 100 million shares. And that was just the NYSE!

The financial news outlets immediately picked up on the story, and reports began to fly around on television and on the Internet. At 10:15, the damage assessment was finalized. During its brief liberation in the market, Power Peg had routed approximately 4 million trade executions in 154 stocks, trading more than 397 million shares. Knight had a net long position in 80 different stocks worth $3.5 billion, and a net short position in 74 different stocks worth $3.15 billion.

By 10:30, Knight's own stock began to plummet. Executives at Knight – with their CEO on the way to the office – began having conversations with regulators and the individual exchanges about cancelling the trades executed by Power Peg. Joyce made it into the office on crutches by noon, and at 12:30 he was officially informed by Niederauer of the NYSE that that Power Peg's trades, although unintended, would stand. Under NYSE rules, they could not be cancelled.

Different exchanges have different rules for allowing trade cancelations. At the NYSE, the trading range must be between 20% and 30% off the opening market price. In Knight's case, the issue was volume, not price. With very few exceptions, none of Power Peg's transactions had moved the stocks more than 10% away from the opening price, which meant that the cancellation rules did not apply. After further review, six of the 140 NYSE-traded securities that Power Peg had traded met the criteria, and those six were cancelled.

It wasn't the news that Joyce was hoping for, to be sure, so he called Mary Schapiro, the Chairman of the SEC. He pleaded his case, explaining that it had been a computer malfunction and that Knight should not be responsible. Sympathetic as she might have been, Schapiro informed Joyce that it was between Knight and the New York Stock Exchange. The SEC had no authority to overrule the NYSE and she was unable to help.

When that Hail Mary (literally) didn't work, another truth came to light. Knight had a $7 billion position in various stocks. Other market participants knew that too, and at some point, Knight had to unload their holdings. Given the massive position, when the time came for them to buy and sell, prices would start moving all around. Wall Street smelled blood in the water, and it was coming from Jersey City.

By the time the market closed on August 1, Knight traders had managed to sell off a big chunk of their stocks. The total position was whittled down to $4.6 billion, which meant that they'd successfully sold off more than $2 billion of their holdings. But another problem still remained - the firm lacked the regulatory capital to hold such a large position, and the clock was ticking. Stocks settled three days after the trade date, which meant that Joyce had three days to either find a buyer for the absurdly large position or figure a way borrowing money to finance the stocks. He started working his Rolodex, calling the large investment banks, knowing that he needed help if Knight was going to stay alive.

In the same way that a buyer of a large block of stock wants a discount for buying the full amount, so, too, would a potential buyer of Knight's massive position. Bids filtered in from market participants and hovered around an 8% to 9% discount from the market's closing prices, far more than the discount Joyce expected. On that $4.6 billion block of stock, a 9% discount amount to $414 million.

Knight then approached Goldman Sachs to buy the portfolio and was shown a bid at a 5% discount. The price from Goldman was better, but it was still going to cost Knight $230 million. It was still a massive commission to pay on the sale, but Knight was up against a wall and they didn't have time to shop around for a better deal.

Meanwhile, Knight tried to arrange emergency funding from JP Morgan to help keep them afloat, but even with an existing credit line in place, they were still dragging their feet. Joyce then received a call from Richard Handler, the CEO of Jeffries who was on vacation in Italy, who told the embattled Joyce that he'd be able to help him out. Handler arranged, through the Jeffries' stock loan desk, the additional funding that Knight needed.

Before the start of the trading day on Thursday, August 2nd, Knight sold off its positions and took the massive loss. While they had about $365 million in cash and liquidity on hand at the time, the losses were still well in excess of that amount. The $200 million they'd lost on cutting their position from $7 billion down to $4.6 billion was just the tip of that iceberg, Power Peg lost money buying on the offered side and selling on the bid side, and they took a hit selling their remaining positions. All told, the firm was looking at a shortfall of approximately $440 million. That was money that they did not have. Taking the losses was a foregone conclusion; there was no way around it. The other foregone conclusion was that they needed a massive capital infusion if they had any hope of staying in business.

On that Thursday, Knight issued a press release as a way of explaining what had happened. They hoped that by coming out immediately it would quell investor fears and cauterize the gash that was bleeding. "Knight experienced a technology issue at the open of trading at the NYSE yesterday," the press release stated. "This issue was related to Knight's installation of trading software and resulted in Knight sending numerous erroneous orders in NYSE-listed securities into the market." It wasn't really a story at that point, as every major financial media outlet had already told and re-told the story countless times.

What it did do, however, was suggest to the Street that the blood they smelled in the water was getting closer. Citadel, a vulture hedge fund with a reputation for swooping in to feast on dying companies, put an offer on the table to provide financing to get them through the weekend, much like Jefferies had offered, and faxed over a term sheet. However the terms were usurious and Joyce declined the offer. It was, quite frankly, an insult to Knight. Thank you, but no thank you.

The insults, however, weren't limited to low-ball offers. Many of Knight's most important clients – including TD Ameritrade, Vanguard, Fidelity Investments, Scottrade, E-Trade, and Pershing, among others – stopped routing orders through Knight. Many of the original roundtable partners weren't so happy with their seat at the table anymore. Without the order flow from their major customers, Knight's money problems only worsened.

Virtu Financial, an electronic trading firm that specialized in high-frequency trading, approached Knight with the equivalent of a life ring being thrown to a drowning man. They were interested in merging, or some type of partnership with Knight. Details of the proposal weren't terribly specific, but given their situation, it seemed like a pretty good offer. It would allow Knight to stay solvent, if nothing else.

Then Citadel came back again. They had flown in a team on Friday to do due diligence over the weekend and, at the last minute on Sunday afternoon, the submitted an offer. Citadel offered to loan Knight $500 million but required an 80% ownership of Knight Hotspot and 10% of Knight itself. Knight needed equity, not more debt, and Hotspot alone was worth $250 million – giving Citadel effectively a $200 million asset for a $500 million loan. That offer, too, was declined without much discussion.

Then, on Monday, August 4, a deal was struck between Knight and a consortium of banks that included Jeffries, Blackstone, TD Ameritrade, Stephens, Stifel Nicolaus, and GETCO. Knight would get $400 million in cash, and the consortium received preferred shares with the option to buy Knight's common shares at $1.50 apiece; shares that could be converted to a 73% ownership in Knight's. In this deal, shareholders would be diluted by about 70%, but Knight would remain independent. It was time for Knight to accept the reality that they were living on borrowed time. The rescue seemed to be complete and the matter was settled. However, Knight would not remain independent for long.

By November, Knight's stock price was hovering around $2.50 a share, which meant the firms who had saved the dying company saw a nice profit – $1.00 a share – if they chose to exercise their options. And they would be happy to do so. It would be quick cash in a relatively short period of time.

So on November 27, Knight was back in play. Virtu Financial once again proposed to buy Knight, this time upping their offer to $3.20 share, all in cash. At the same time, GETCO, a Chicago-based high-frequency trading firm, was contemplating their own bid. They were already a market-maker in 500 different NYSE stocks, and they relied heavily on Knight's algorithms for trade executions. They estimated they could save between $90 and $110 million annually just by combining their operations with those of Knight.

GETCO immediately submitted a bid for Knight following Virtu. The new bid – a combination of cash and stock – started off at $3.50 a share, the climbed up to $3.60 and eventually landed at $3.70 a share. Their plan was to carve up Knight and sell off the individual components to pay off the debt they'd incur. The offers were put to a vote by Knight's shareholders and a majority agreed that GETCO was the better option - Knight Capital Group was officially sold to GETCO. The firm that had ridden the technology wave to the top found themselves a victim of technology in the end.

*   *   *

Throughout his tenure as CEO at Knight, Thomas Joyce openly discussed what were deemed to be the most "significant risks," both with board members and with the employees. When one employee once asked what Joyce saw as the biggest risk to the firm's well being, Joyce suggested that a rogue trader was, to his mind, the biggest threat they faced. It never occurred to him that an algorithm running in the computer system would turn out to be the rogue trader he so feared.

As for the IT employee who installed the new software – or who failed to install the software – the firm took precautions to preserve both his privacy and his own personal safety. He was never publicly outed by the company and he was placed on twenty-four-hour-a-day suicide watch. Every evening after work, a

Knight employee would accompany him home and stay with him until he returned to the office the next morning.

At its core, though, what happened at Knight was more than just human error. Yes, the human component was a major contributing factor, but it wasn't the only one. The disaster that was wrought in the first five minutes of the trading day on August 1 was a software problem. The ensuing 35 minutes, however, were a catastrophic failure of risk management. It was more an institutional problem than the fault of any individual. Somehow Knight as a company didn't have adequate controls in place to prevent the erroneous orders, nor did they have the necessary controls to ensure the proper deployment of new computer code, nor did they choose to shut the connection to the NYSE down when the trades were mounting.

Of course, the failure of the firm's risk-management policies is manifested in the fact that they didn't have a kill switch in place to shut down the system. That would have solved the problem shortly after it became a problem in the first place. And it could have been a very simple algorithmic expression for a programmer to write: IF the daily volume reaches a certain level, THEN shut it down. Alternatively, substituting any number of factors for "daily volume" would have had equally beneficial results: profit/loss, market exposure, firm's capital. Pick one. Any of those would have substantially eased the pain Knight experienced. Perhaps the IT staff was unfairly singled out for their arrogance.

The SEC began an investigation in Knight's trading practices and their risk management policies just days after the Power Peg incident. They would later say in their final report that the firm was in direct violation of the SEC Market Access Rule and that Knight lacked reasonable risk-management procedures. The merger with Getco was completed on July 1st, so Knight officially no longer existed. Tom Joyce resigned his position as CEO on July 3, 2013 and retired. Senior technology executives were purged from the firm's employee roster, while others were reassigned to other positions within the company. Knight was then fined $12 million by the SEC.

Walter Raquet, the man who originally conceived of Knight Capital Group, would say of the Power Peg affair, "It couldn't have happened under Kenny's and my watch. We had so many controls that something like that could never have happened." And even though it's easy for him to Monday Morning Quarterback the situation, you have to wonder if his technological insight and forward-thinking would have thought that something could go so drastically wrong with firm's computer systems. After all, the firm had fundamentally changed in the ten years since Raquet had left and the systems were only as good as the people who programmed them.

On December 23, 2012, the IntercontinentalExchange Group, which now owns the NYSE Euronext, filed a plan to offer all of their member firms a kill switch as a way of preventing another Power Peg incident. Under that plan, member firms would have the option of pre-setting trade thresholds that blocked the firms' orders when thresholds were reached. Two other stock trading platforms – BATS and Direct Edge – already had a kill switch function for their members.

Shortly thereafter, Power Peg was officially erased once and for all. The program was completely deleted from all of Knight's servers, prompting a senior executive to announce ceremoniously, "Power Peg is now dead." Never again would it be able to rise up and go rogue. The person who woke Power Peg up from its hibernation was never named, as Thomas Joyce continues to this day his policy of protecting the privacy of the employees involved in the incident.

Because algorithms are nothing more than a set of instructions that a computer follows, traders must still monitor their executions and keep close tabs on what the algorithms are doing. An algorithm is only as good as the person who writes it and there are many possible alternatives to the final outcome of Knight's disastrous flow.

IF Knight's systems administrators had deleted Power Peg in 2003 when they were supposed to, THEN Power Peg would not have created the mess it did. IF Knight had procedures in place to review the deployment of the SMARS update, THEN they would have caught the missing code on the eighth server. IF someone at Knight had paid attention to the error messages they received on August 1st, THEN Power Peg could have been turned off before it started trading. IF the flag that turned Power Peg on hadn't been recycled, THEN Power Peg never would have woken up. IF a kill switch had been installed, THEN the losses would have been minimized.

That's a lot of IF statements to be sure, but perhaps the most pointed IF-THEN came from Larry Tabb of the Tabb Group. His words, expressed as an algorithm, were quite damning of the system as a whole: "If this happens to one of the most sophisticated players in the market, then we really need to rethink our overall market structure."

CONCLUSION

I n *The Bonfire of the Vanities*, author Tom Wolfe collectively referred to those who work on Wall Street as "the masters of the universe." While it's a tongue-in-cheek comment on the self-importance that many traders ascribe to themselves, it's also an apt description of this elite segment of the population. A microscopic percentage of the people living on Earth work in the financial industry, yet many of them have the power to affect the financial markets on a global scale.

We're told that with great power comes great responsibility, and make no mistake, the power held by those buying and selling the world's financial instruments is great. The vast majority of traders on Wall Street both recognize and appreciate that power, treating it with the respect it deserves. They are, by and large, an honest group seeking to make a living – albeit a very comfortable one – while making money for those they serve. But as we've seen, there are those, too, who represent a darker side of the profession.

Rogue traders are often able to stay one step ahead of the game, at least for a while, constantly finding the loopholes and flaws in the system that will keep their illegal activities secret for just a little longer. Risk management at financial institutions has historically reacted to rogue trading events and evolved because of them. In some cases, those reactions meant increasing the level of risk monitoring; in others, it simply meant paying attention to the obvious warning signs that were present all along.

Regardless of the reasons for the changes, the end result was usually the same: The financial institution was forced to examine how it did business on a day-to-day basis and to figure out a way to prevent the same thing from happening again. And that's exactly the problem. Fishermen know that casting a lure to where they saw a fish is where it *was*, not where it *is* currently. By changing the policies and procedures in reaction to an event, banks are paying attention to what has already happened instead of predicting what might happen next. Over the past 30 years, banks have generally stayed one step behind the next rogue trading event, making it even easier for less-than-scrupulous traders to ply their trades in relative professional safety.

In the case of David Heuwetter of Drysdale, we saw the seeds sown for the most widely-used investment innovation of the late twentieth century - leverage. The use of leverage not only increased profits, but also risk-taking in the financial system. While leverage has made many traders very, very wealthy, it has also brought down some of the biggest names in finance: Long Term Capital Management, Bear Stearns, Lehman Brothers, MF Global, and the list can go on. Regardless of how you view leverage, after Drysdale Securities collapsed, the new rules and regulations that were introduced were supposed to prevent anything similar from happening again. They didn't.

Howard Rubin, though he denied the practice, made the phrase "hiding the tickets in the drawer" the running joke on Wall Street for years thereafter. That same phrase became an amorphous fear amongst Wall Street executives, who thought that more traders might be doing the same thing. What Rubin could not deny, however, was the fact that he engaged in what Merrill Lynch executives termed "significant unauthorized activity." Rubin's defense was that his supervisors knew what he was doing all along and the Merrill trading system couldn't properly price the securities he was trading.

In the case of Joe Jett of Kidder Peabody, the rogue element was simply a flaw in the firm's accounting system. The trade processing system was programmed so that it couldn't tell the difference between an actual trade and a quasi-trade in STRIPS and recon transactions that settled many days in the future. The genius of his plan, if you want to call it that, is that he was able to book such a sheer volume of trades that it made his "strategy" appear valid and lucrative. In reality, it was not. Jett saw a flaw in a system and was willing to exploit it.

The rogue trading story of Nick Leeson and Barings was, at its core, a lesson in the separation of duties. Leeson had a broad and powerful role within the company – he was responsible for both the trading and back-office personnel in the far-off Singapore office. Senior management would not challenge him because they feared their questions appeared naïve. When Leeson siphoned money into the error account, there was nobody to oversee what he was doing.

Brian Hunter, the man who owned nearly 40% of the total outstanding natural gas futures contracts while at Amaranth, believed that extremely large positions gave him control of the market. Like a retail store that sells products for lower prices and makes up the profit difference on volume, Hunter relied on sheer position size as the foundation of his strategy. He was even able to circumvent position size limits at the NYMEX just by moving over to the ICE exchange. But his positions became so large that any attempt to book profits resulted in the natural gas market declining. In a perfect catch-22, he'd single-handedly driven up the price to the point that when he chose to sell, he moved the market lower.

The case of Jerome Kerviel at Société Générale was one of management simply falling asleep at the wheel. The bank's practice of appointing under-qualified middle managers to assignments was looked at as a training exercise for future executives. So when

Kerviel's new manager took over, it was incredibly easy for the rogue trader to take advantage. Eric Cordelle simply scanned the bottom lines of reports to make sure that the numbers were in line with expectations; his lack of understanding of what Kerviel was actually doing meant that he couldn't question the trader's actions. That ignorance allowed Kerviel to manipulate and exceed his risk limits on a massive scale.

The American justice system recognizes the importance of undue influence when allowing a judge to determine guilt or innocence, but the board in charge of LIBOR – perhaps the single most important interest rate in the world – did not have sufficient oversight to prevent a bank's submitters from being influenced by its own trading positions. By granting proprietary traders access to the submitters, there was an immediate and obvious conflict of interest. Traders have an incentive to make money; submitters have a duty to accurately report the bank's lending rates. Tom Hayes was able to build a network of submitters to the LIBOR board whom he coaxed into sending rates that would benefit his own trading positions. When profit and duty collided, the result was the LIBOR scandal.

The voters of Orange County, California, learned a lesson that many others have learned over the years, namely the fact that you can't get something for nothing. While it's certainly appealing to find the perfect investment offering high returns without inherent risk, the search is today's equivalent to the Medieval alchemists searching for the chemical formula to turn lead into gold. It just doesn't exist. And while Robert Citron might have claimed ignorance in the investment world, he was trying to keep an impossible campaign promise: finance the government and increase services without requiring more taxes. The only way to fulfill that promise was through high-risk investments, a strategy that backfired on a monumental scale.

Toshihide Iguchi from Daiwa Bank fell victim to a common quality assigned to tragic heroes in drama, namely the concept of hubris. So great was the perceived fallout from losing face – or suffering a personal embarrassment – that he couldn't publicly admit to a loss on a bad trade. He exploited Daiwa's lack of internal controls that allowed him to settle his own trading positions, which only increased his losses. It was a vicious cycle that snowballed until it finally crashed into him.

"Mr. Copper," or Yasuo Hamanaka, tried to corner the copper market, a goal some see as the ultimate trade in the financial markets. In theory, he who controls the supply also controls the price. If a trader were able to control enough supply in the warehouses, he could control the price, and the potential profits could be astronomical. But there are always other factors working against those seeking to corner a market, and Hamanaka found them out the hard way.

The group known as the NAB 4 found loopholes in their bank's trade processing system and used that knowledge to input false trades that showed they were making money. The result was a colossal failure of risk-management that should have caught their rogue activity.

In what might best be called a common theme among rogue traders, the London Whale is a story of traders assuming more risk than they're authorized. Internal risk controls are supposed to be based on well-defined limits, and they exist for a reason. But smart rogue traders can find ways around risk limits to justify just about anything. When these traders were given free reign to ramp-up their positions, "defending the position" because paramount to everything else.

Finally, we saw the rise of the machines in Knight Capital Group's Power Peg. In today's world, the financial market's reliance on technology is absolute. And given the ability of a computer to process stock trades in milliseconds, it only makes sense for computers to dominate the trading floor. But the algorithm is only as good as the instructions that it's given and because a computer cannot think for itself, it has no way of understanding when it's not doing what it's supposed to be do. The emotionless machine continued to wreak havoc until a human stepped in to stop it.

Philosopher George Santayana famously said in 1905, "Those who cannot remember the past are condemned to repeat it." His words were answered, almost as famously, by author Kurt Vonnegut years later, who said, "I've got news for Mr. Santayana: we're doomed to repeat the past no matter what. That's what it is to be alive."

Vonnegut was never accused of being overly optimistic in his views of humanity, but the rogue trader stories in this collection bear out the truth of his statement. Every rogue trader that comes along – and I want to be clear, they are only a small minority of the traders out there – thinks that he has perfected the system, that he is smarter than those that came before him. Like any criminal, he is convinced that he figured out the perfect, fool-proof system that cannot fail. He is a master of the universe. A rogue universe that he himself has created, but a master of that universe nevertheless.

And perhaps there is another rogue trader out there right now. After all, if he's doing it right, he's making money and not getting caught. And it's only when he gets caught that it suddenly becomes a news story. Time has a way of catching up to all of us, rogue traders included.

More importantly, however, is the prevention of rogue trading in the first place. It would be easy to suggest that human greed is the root of all rogue trading, but we have seen examples where greed wasn't the primary motivator. Power Peg was a computer without any understanding of human traits and the Orange County bankruptcy resulted from a man who had arguably the best of intentions for the people of Orange County. So if we can't chalk it all up to greed, what, then, is needed to prevent future episodes?

The honest answer is that the onus falls on financial executives. Just as an elected official must answer to his constituents, corporate executives must be held accountable for the actions of those that they employ. We've heard all too often that a corporation is too large for a CEO to know what every employee is doing, and that is true. It doesn't absolve them, however, from the responsibility of ensuring that their lieutenants employ adequate risk-management and oversight. If an employer chooses to hire those who view themselves as masters of the universe, that employer needs to understand the risks inherent in giving such a high degree of self-esteem the keys to the kingdom. That ego needs constant strengthening, and for a few traders, the only way to get that power is through illegal, immoral, or unethical methods.

Yes, to err is human, and mistakes are an inevitable part of humanity. However, by reacting to rogue trading as opposed to proactively hindering the rogue actions of the future, corporate leaders are not doing enough. Shareholders need to hold the men and women who are in charge accountable. Institutions that are too large to incorporate proper oversight and avoid unauthorized risk-taking, are, by definition, too large to manage.

ABOUT THE AUTHOR

S cott Skyrm is an Executive Vice President at Curvature Securities, LLC and has worked in fixed-income markets as a trader, salesman, trading desk manager his entire career. His previous books are *The Money Noose — Jon Corzine and The Collapse of MF Global (June 2013) and Rogue Traders* (April 2014). He is well-known in the financial press at: The Wall Street Journal, Financial Times, The New York Times, Bloomberg News, Market News Service, and CNBC. He holds an M.S. in Economics; B.A. in Economics Lehigh University and currently resides in New Canaan, CT.